The 7 Steps

of an Effective Sales Call

Om Namah Shivaya

The 7 Steps

of an Effective Sales Call

AN F.M.C.G. SALESMAN'S BIBLE

Rajul Chaturvedi

PARTRIDGE

To order additional copies of this book, contact
Partridge India
000 800 10062 62
orders.india@partridgepublishing.com

www.partridgepublishing.com/india

Contents

Preface

"All successful sales people do many right things that need to be done during a sales call but if they do it knowingly & in the right sequence, they can be much more effective"

We live in a changed world today and lot of things in a sales environment have changed drastically in the past some years. Technology is slowly taking over, processes have changed & ways to do business are changing. What has still not changed is the large traditional brick & mortar or mom and pop retail store landscape & ever increasing number of traditional trade outlets and a vast majority of them in the developing countries & fast growing economies like India & China. On the other hand E commerce is making rapid inroads and sales is going quite technical with palm tops and hand held devices. I believe they are still far from denting the mom & pop stores to a serious level. Most things today in business can be automated and handled via technology, but sales is one of those things that still requires real people & people skills, hence i believe that the old fashioned sales call is still quite in relevance.

Sales is like eating food, one cannot live without eating but the dishes can change with time

Starting 'Right'

During my early sales days i was quite sceptical about some concepts of selling & i thought that selling was an art. Time passed by and i realized that it was quite like a science which was to be learned, understood and practiced. There were no formal institutes or training centres for salesmen when i started working in India in the late 80's but I thank my stars for being able to start with an organization which was an institution in itself specially for the salesmen. I do not know where i would have been in life without learning the kind of sales basics & selling skills i learnt there. The organization not only showed me the right way but also made me realize that if i get the basic concepts right and structural efficiencies in place, it all works like a well lubricated machinery. I was sceptical about many concepts that were taught in theory but just implemented them sincerely without questioning any and believe me they worked like magic in the field. I saw the power of the structured call made in the way they taught me, i was not only respected in the market then but till today retailers and people remember me and my visits. The various techniques when applied made the retailer dance to my tunes. My first company *Gillette®* truly believed in investing in training its people hard and that paid immensely to them as well as the employees.

I have worked with some of the best companies in the world *(Gillette®, Duracell®, Henkel & United biscuits)*, some amazing people & great environments and have always felt that the right start with the right platform is so very important for anyone. I was a small town boy in the world of top class professionals and was armed just with my never say die attitude, immense confidence and the determination to reach somewhere. I had no formal or professional degree in management or sales and when i started i just had one thought in my mind 'How can i be the best sales guy amongst all'.

Coming from a small town in the state of western Uttar Pradesh (Saharanpur) in India and straight into the cut throat corporate metropolitan hustle bustle of Delhi, I was clueless on how to start and where to start and how to adjust to the pace. I am grateful to some of the amazing managers that i worked under specially to start with Joginder Pal Singh an extremely simple and straightforward sales person i met during my initial days of coming to terms with a sales career, who taught me the baby steps & then the stylish and genius Ranu Kawatra, FMS Delhi (Cadbury's, Gillette®, Duracell®, Pearson) & not to forget 'the boss', the firebrand, flamboyant & dashing Pradeep pant from Jamnalal Bajaj (Nestle, Gillette®, Fonterra, Mondelez) to mention the most as, they were such an influence, personally & professionally and have played a crucial role in making a difference to my career and personality.

All that i was armed with in the name of skills when i arrived in the big metropolitan capital of India, was my extremely positive attitude, willingness to learn, indulge and adopt to anything that could make me successful. I was always able to get along and maintain a good relationship with almost everyone in any team i worked with and specially with some of the big name in the industry, just because of these simple traits that i had. Be it language, words, mannerisms, traits or skills i made it a point to learn & practice every bit i could. I believe that most of my managers first liked me more for my 'amazing' positive attitude, great energy and never say die attitude. I am sure that none of the people who have worked with me would have ever seen my face without a smile or me low on energy, they used to ask me how do i keep myself so full of energy and smiling all the time. I never ever said no to any task given to me even if i didn't know how to do it. I always felt that let's take this up as a challenge and find a way to do it rather than refuse for the fear of failing or not knowing. I was always sure that i will be able to do it and did it successfully most of the times. The other big thing was that i was able to learn more new things than people who refused to take new challenges or go out of their comfort zone to do anything.

Importance of basics

Having been an integral part of some of the best companies & best brands launched into India, i have realized that they too have learnt the hard way. However great people you have, however big brands you have, whatever big investment you put in, still nothing might help if the basics are not in place. You still have to go thru the rigmarole of creating a robust infrastructure of reaching the humongous millions of outlets all over the world, along with addressing the complexities of territories, states, cities, towns, villages, languages, cultures & above all people. People were and are still the single most important factor and the human touch and relations form the core of it.

Another important factor, the biggest marketing guru's & companies have paid heavily by being ignorant of the frontline or being obsessed with the brand, investment, size or momentum or have forgot the human angle. They have ignored the basics leading to creating unforeseen weak links, the infrastructure cracking under pressure and ultimately end up paid a heavy price many a times. They may blame all failures on different marketing strategies making elaborate & fancy presentations but the fact also may be that they have failed to connect with their own sales force to make it successful. I have seen many great marketing plans fail and then sales pulling them thru with their sheer skills to handle the trade and people, such is the power.

It's all about people, Trained & Skilful one's

So why is training the sales force so important? or is it important at all. As mentioned already that in spite of having world class brands, great systems, great management team, great marketing team if you don't have a well trained frontline sales team, you might find it harder to succeed. The sales team of any organization is not only the ambassador of the organization but the one which drives revenue & profitability, get that right. They can mess up the best of the marketing and sales plans if they are not skilful enough in execution of the same. Best of the marketing and sales plans require execution finesse and if the frontline falters there, the whole organization may suffer. Organizations are about people and the organizations which do not invest in training, educating & upgrading their people, are most likely to have a tough time fighting competition and being successful.

So get the basics right from day one & never ignore the people and people skills, they are the ones who can & will make you sail through.

Now why steps of a call or a structured call at all? Extremely important for everyone to understand is that the sales team comes from varied backgrounds & cultures (professionally & personally). The understanding of the business of each individual is different due to their past different experiences or way of operations. Their way of thinking and approach to sales and selling situations might be exactly the opposite of what you perceive due to their personality traits product nature, market environment or lack of any formal training to sell. So in order to get them into one single string of understanding and operating, any organization needs to introduce them to the organization's own way of doing business. This will not only get them to think and act alike but also inculcate the organization culture in them. Once that is done we also want them to perform and achieve similar & uniform results. That is only possible if everyone is trained the same way and they are taught to speak the same language, follow the same ethics and think alike.

Sales people are not selling machines, they are human and need a lot of caring, motivation and support. Organizations who take them as machines and evaluate them only on their outcome versus what they pay to them (without any other inputs) have got it all wrong. They are bound to break down and stop delivering sooner than they think. If any organization does not adopt training & upgrading its people as a philosophy or religion, it will never work for them and they might never know what was wrong in their products, approach or strategy. Training is a constant process and has to go on the results will follow. The way of life for organizations should be train, motivate, monitor, re-train, motivate, train and retain the best.

I have mentioned earlier also that the frontline salesmen are the arms & hands of any organization. The weaker they are the worst it gets, the skilful they are the better will be the results. Any organization which has invested constantly in training, educating & updating their people (specially frontline), has never failed. Any organization which has ignored investing in the training & skill development of their sales force have struggled.

Make no mistake 'The salesman is the sole bread earner of the organization' the rest of the organization team exists only to support him do that.

How did i choose sales as a career

So those were the time of becoming doctor's & engineer's and each and every household was gunning for these two career's for their children. I somehow found myself unfit for these two and wanted something with more excitement & action (I was not that inclined academically). During my schooling and college days i used to travel to Delhi (India's capital) and do small odd jobs in selling to experience some type of a career and make some bucks. I found selling quite exciting & with the added bonus of meeting different people, interacting with them, exchanging thoughts on various topics, travelling far & wide which were much more exciting than attending boring coaching classes for engineering, medical and finally being in an office 9 to 6. I realized that i was excellent with communication skills and also connected instantly with people (Most complimented me for my spoken English and how i could express myself and things so well). I also loved to listen to and share real life experiences & stories and wanted to do things differently, my way. Later in the years when it came to choosing a career, when i looked back and analyzed what i really loved, 'Sales' was the instant answer. It had all the elements i enjoyed and were required for in this career, so be it.

The Gillette® philosophy

I will quote once again the classic example of *'The Gillette® company'* in India which is known for creating one of the finest army of frontline sales people & managers most of whom now have gone on to become CEO's & Directors in leading MNC's the world over.

The company was created in 1901 by a travelling salesman called 'King C. Gillette®' who was an extremely successful sales person himself. He knew & believed in the importance and power of a skilled & motivated sales person. The philosophy of emphasis on training and investing in constantly upgrading it's sales persons resulted in churning out high quality & skilful sales force over decades. Investing in sharpening selling & other skills of its sales force was practiced as a religion all over, which made it one of the greatest organizations of all times, the world over.

Gillette® was one of the very few companies in those days which always had a full-fledged sales training department & a robust training infrastructure in place which was responsible for a trained, monitored & highly motivated sales team 365 days a year. They not only survived without any much media in the cut throat world of shaving products but also became market leaders wherever they went. They always had the best possible shaving products but the cutting edge always came from the quality of people that they had, skilled, motivated & unbeatable.

Gillette® recruited the best and made sure that they bread the best. They were always envied for the kind of field force that they had and their people coveted in the industry. They were able to create one of the best distributed & merchandised brand in India without paying even a single penny to the retailer for visibility. Their sales force had the best of the relations with the trade and channel partners and it was a one big family, always. They were an example even to the best of organizations operating in India for creating the most visible brand in Indian market without paying even a penny for it. Their sales call & merchandising training programs are a folk lore in sales circles around India. Their way of operation is a case study in leading management colleges across India.

For more on Gillette® read -

1) "King C. Gillette®, The Man and His Wonderful Shaving Device" by Russell Adams (1978), published by Little Brown & Co. of Boston, Massachusetts, U.S.

2) *McKibben, Gordon (1998). Cutting Edge: Gillette's® Journey to Global Leadership. Harvard Business School Press. ISBN 0-87584-725-0.*

3) The Gillette® Company History (thefundinguniverse.com)

Importance of fundamentals

The most important thing to understand is that whatever happens to the country environment, sales environment, company environment, people environment and local issues the basics of any business remain the mostly the same. Any individual or company with strong basics is the one most likely to succeed. So get the facts right and thinking straight, establish yourself with strong basics, get the basics right get the fundamentals right.

It might not be fun establishing the fundamentals and on the contrary can be quite boring and monotonous most of the times. It's sheer hard work but that's the first thing you will need to do for a successful future & foundation. So if there are times when you need to be compared with competition, the organization with the fundamentals in place is the one which will most probably stay put & succeed. It will give you that additional edge to fight it out and stay there to succeed.

Concentrate on the fundamentals and you will see that it becomes so easy. Ninety nine percent of the things will fall in place if you get the fundamentals right. Whatever the situation, whichever the company and whatever the people if they do not get the fundamentals of any business right, it's going to be really tough for them to succeed.

At some point of time in a sales career many people do ask some important questions to themselves.

Why are some people more successful than the others?

What is different that they do?

How can i make a difference in my performance?

What are the basic things that i need to do?

What are the basic mistakes that i need to address immediately?

Good you thought that!

The early you ask these questions to yourself the early success you will achieve. These are questions about future and career and need to be answered with utmost thoughtfulness. It's also about having a smooth & successful career and leaving a legacy about yourself of which you can be proud of yourself once you retire from work.

The answer is that they first need to understand the importance of knowing the basics, how things work, what are the factors that affect their performance, what are the steps that they need to take to correct them. They also need to understand the importance of a structured approach to doing things and specially selling if they have chosen sales as a career. They need to clearly understand that sales is not an art, it an science which needs to be studied learnt, understood & practiced.

For many successful sales people, reading through the various chapters of this book they will realize how practical and real it is. They will also realize that whatever has been written has been practiced by them during their calls at some point of time or the other. Many will also realize that 'yes' lot of things were missing and they could have been more effective had they known them beforehand.

Remember 'you are the biggest barrier to your success'. What you are today is always the sum of your past, current and what you wish to become in the future. The objective of this book is to help you know about making a difference to your own self and be a success story.

This is not a theory book as i am not a PHD or from any IVY league. This book has also not risen out of any high end laboratory experiments. This book has been written by a salesman himself, from accounts of his own personal experiences arisen out of thousands of sales calls that he has personally made and situations that he has personally faced or handled. This has been written with the same spirit that i always had as an sales person from inside, simple, honest & factual.

The most important part of sales career is to be an 'Excellent Sales person' first and to enjoy & love this job while doing it, success will follow. I have been selling for the past 25 years and believe me that I not only feel excited every time i do it today also but also still learn something from it every time i do it. I still have the same passion for selling that i had 25 years back when i started selling and fell in love with this career.

It's a tough job but the good news is that sales in not rocket science and it is all easily learnable if you are willing to.

Chapter 1

Develop Your Personality

What is the definition of personality?

**One's personality is a typical way
of conducting one's mannerism's,
thinking, behaviour, actions,
speaking and carrying himself
that make a person unique
or different from others.**

So, if someone says that someone has a "good personality"
we generally mean that the person is likeable, interesting

and pleasant to be with. In fact, it is well established that approximately 80 percent of your success and happiness will be a result of how effectively you interact with others. Ultimately, it is your overall personality that determines whether people will be attracted to you, or stay away from you. Your personality reflects what you are and people who meet you for the first time or for a short time, judge you by how you carry yourself and what your mannerisms are, all this determines your personality.

Your personality changes many times during your life due to various reasons. Although you may not notice it happening but it does as you grow but some older behaviours may become ingrained or dominant. The key to improving your personality is knowing your weaknesses, shortcomings and changing some behaviours or attributes to reinforce good personality traits and limit negative personality traits. For this it is important to know and realize as to what needs improvement and why. Having done that self analysis, it's time that you act and start make amendments immediately.

Your overall personality plays an extremely crucial role in your sales call and many a times can make or break it even before you attempt it. I am mentioning some important aspects of any personality which are a must to be looked into.

Communication

A sales career is all about communicating effectively. It not only constitutes of the language but also pronunciation, voice modulation, punctuation and the right words. Invest in learning languages like English which is widely spoken internationally apart from being the chosen way to communicate specially in developing countries around the world.

The power of effective communication is that it brings out whatever is inside you in such a way that it seems real and convincing. An effective communication can create war between two countries or bring them to peace, win elections or move masses to do anything, such is the power of communication.

Communication is also not restricted to content, it is also about telling stories. Everyone wants to hear stories (especially if you are in sales) and if you are one who can narrate it well, you are always welcome and listened to. Many companies specially develop sales stories to communicate the message of the product.

For effective communication, use simple words, speak slowly & clearly, be brief (until asked for an explanation) use gestures & look into his eyes. You have to make sure that you are understood. Do not blame the other person for not understanding. Instead find ways to clarify or re phrase what you have said. Speak clearly, take pauses ask questions make sure that the listener is understanding what you are saying or trying to convey.

There are whole books on this subject hence i will not write much, perhaps in my next book.

Personal Grooming

An extremely crucial aspect of a sales guy, if you are not groomed well, consider the sales lost anyways and the career not for you. Everyone likes to talk to a smart, well groomed guy & if you are not one, the call has ended even before it began. You have to look fresh, smell good and dress well always. It is all about how you take care of yourself & how you look. Your clothes, your tie, your shoes and that special hair cut (not a wild one) can make all the difference. You have to look great in every call and every bit of you has to be looking great. Every inch of you should seem professional and neat.

Personal hygiene

Another important aspect of your personality which directly affects your sales call is personal hygiene. Personal hygiene constitutes of bathing daily, brushing your teeth regularly, cutting your hairs regularly, cutting your nails regularly and smelling fresh. No one wants to speak to a guy who looks untidy, smells bad, is chewing tobacco or looks exhausted already. Your hairs have to be cut & combed neatly, your nails have to be clipped recently, you have to smell good, you have to be shaved or if you have a beard it should be nicely kept & well maintained. No harm if you wash your face after every some calls to look fresh. An exhausted looking and untidy person will get no business.

Dressing sense

Your clothes are a big indicator of your personality, what you perceive yourself to be and ultimately reflects your thought process. Formal dressing is important whenever you are on work, never take the customer / client lightly. Be it Friday or Saturday if you are on a call be dressed formally, i recommend that. No bold colours or prints, new styles or fancy dressing it has to be an absolute professional statement. Your clothes ironed well, your shoes have to be well polished and shining, your tie bold and formal. Don't take even one day lightly, each moment spent in the market / field has to be taken seriously and formally, do not forget you are at work and that perception about you can make the vital difference. Everyone is watching you be informed.

Personal Health

An extremely important aspect of a sales career, you have to keep yourself healthy. A healthy body will carry you far, you will feel confident, go that extra mile and be able to swim thru any circumstances. If you are sick or coughing or with droopy yellow eyes your customer might not even like to meet you. Your energy is what will energize the sales call so if you are low on energy consider the call to be dead. Make sure that you spend some time for a physical workout routine (At least 4 days a week), eat the right food, drink & smoke in moderation (If you cannot avoid it). Quitting that smoking or refusing that extra drink will take you a long way. If you smoke too much, drink heavily, eating too much of that junk food or indulge in things which keep you away from the required eight hours of sleep you are in for many unseen troubles later in your career. You have to indulge in actions which are detrimental in the wrong run or maybe short term too. Always remember, in this tough journey of life and a demanding career of sales your body is the only thing that will stand by you and help delivering extra. Respect your body and stop abusing it.

Discipline

I consider this one to be the most crucial one as this has really helped me pass unscratched thru so many adverse situations. If you are disciplined in life you already have a great factor for success in place and on your side. I have seen many a great sales guy fail or not able to go any higher as their life was highly undisciplined.

Respect things like being in time every time, informing cancelled appointments, maintaining deadlines in spite of sudden exigencies. Realizing the importance of others time. Getting up early, following a routine of personal and professional lines all fall under being disciplined.

Companies really respect & value disciplined employees. Even if you feel at times 'does this really make a difference' the answer is 'It makes a huge difference'. You may not notice it but there would definitely be many who will admire your discipline, as it is not an easy thing. Your life will be much simpler and easy if you are able to discipline yourself.

Monitor yourself

Finally i suggest that you need to consciously work on your personality traits. Sit down and list them down in two categories what you like about yourself and what you want to change about yourself. Separate them by what you want to work upon immediately and what later. Keep a constant watch or take someone into confidence to help monitor or give feedback. Studies about how people learn & grow have shown that when you pay attention to what and how well you are learning, your learning improves many a times. Remembering and applying new knowledge and skills become easier when you keep an eye on your progress while learning something. You know yourself the best, hence easier to diagnose how fast you are learning and where to push yourself.

Join a new organization, class, club, team or group. It is easy to go back into old habits with people who know you already; however, new acquaintances won't have expectations and you may be more successful starting a new behaviour. Remember personalities don't change overnight. Give yourself plenty of time and space to turn behaviour into an improved personality.

Learn to overcome fear and to deal with rejection and failure in order to increase your productivity while saving time and money.

Never forget, You have to
sell yourself first...........

Chapter 2

Traits of Successful Sales People

Positive Attitude

Attitude is everything and a positive attitude can move mountains. Your entire approach to any task changes with a slight attitude change. The classic example is of glass half full or half empty. Your attitude is 100% within your control. There are plenty of things in life that we have no control over, all we can do is control the manner in which we approach the situations & people. Think about it; are you as positive, upbeat and driven on a day full of rejection or criticism as you would be on a highly successful day? I have already mentioned previously also on how great a virtue a positive attitude is.

Communication skills

Successful sales people are great communicators and have a command over what they say. They always have a lot of knowledge to share and create an impression. They are also backed by command of details of what they are selling. They can change their communication style based on circumstances and people they communicate with. They are also full of brilliant stories which they weave into their communication and get their way thru. They can modulate their tone to suit the intensity of the discussion and change the entire coarse of conversation with their communication skills. I have already mentioned about communication in my previous chapter. *I personally rate this the top most one as nothing succeeds this one.*

Patient listeners

Successful sales people are good listeners and do not speak unnecessarily or obstruct when someone is speaking. They realize the importance of hearing out the other person fully to arrive at the right answer. They know the right words, the right tone, the right sentences, where to pause and make the listener dance to their tunes but for all that they make sure that they have heard him fully first. They are keen observers and make sure to incorporate their observations into their communications. They are able to communicate effectively to the customer, what he wants to listen. They are well aware that there is nothing more offending then interrupting a thought process of another individual specially a prospective customer. What they think about you is important as that will influence the buying decision, so how do you know what he thinks about you - Listen to him and most probably you will be able to make out. Listening is a great way to gain valuable real-time insight of customer sentiment.

The Go-getter attitude (Positive Aggression)

That's a must as there is no safe playing in this career. You have to be a go-getter of things and cannot wait for things to happen to you. A Go-getter mentality is something that nobody is really born with, it is rather something that we progressively nurture over time as a result of situations, circumstances, people and our own introspection. It's about being aggressive (Positive aggression) in your approach to situations & issues. It is something that we become as a result of how we have interacted with the world around us for getting the results that we want. And as a result, this Go-getter mentality helps us to go that extra mile, do more and achieve more in life. It of course is not easy to cultivate a Go-Getter mentality if you don't have an upbringing encouraging it. It is all about standing up and taking up the challenge rather than waiting for a situation of comfort or it be thrust on you. It actually takes a lot of courage, energy and effort that a great many people aren't willing to put themselves through. You can call it a aggressive, street-smart, sharp & energetic version of you. The Go-getter enjoys taking risks and pushing boundaries of what others believe is possible. This not only gives them an emotional high but also propels them forward to even greater feats of accomplishment. They are always valued above all weather they succeed in their initiations or fail. *I personally rate this trait right amongst the top one's to have.*

Positive thinker

Successful sales people are positive thinkers, they always look towards the shiny side of things. Positive thinkers never complain instead find solutions about anything and everything. They always focus on the good, have bright ideas and are always encouraging. They have everything good and positive to talk about and would avoid negative discussions. They are full of possibilities and solutions and are approached in all situations by colleagues for solutions and support.

Never take it Personally

Successful sales people never take things personally as they have no ego. Any comment made about them or to them is evaluated on it's merit. They do not react on impulse and keep quite or reserve their statement even if it is a genuinely offending statement. They make their statements in low but firm tones and are honest about their feelings. Their opinions are always honest and will never utter offending statements. They never provoke or indulge in 'give it back' game.

Respect an individual's value & beliefs

Successful sales people are respectful to other people's feelings and give credit for honest and valuable opinion. They never make insulting statements during discussions. They do not actively seek revenge against another person. They will state a point very calmly when required and then listen to the discussion, never impressing upon their opinion. They let other people be with their views and never take a stance against other people's value's and belief's. In an event of heated argument they are the ones who initiate peace or truce.

Do not indulge in Gossip

Successful sales people stay away from the gossip world as for them it involves bitching about people. They are simple at heart and believe in staying away from bitching and other controversies. Their position is of content and they have so much to share or do amongst themselves or with the team that they find no interest in gossip. Their aim in life keeps them away from all possible complicated situations which gossip can land them into. Finally they have less time for any gossip as they have too many things to learn and way too far to go.

Never lie

Lying for anything for a successful sales person is a strict 'No, No' never ever lie is their simple motto, be honest and straightforward is the only thing they would like to practice. Retailers are ready to listen to all kind of stories but not lies. In fact they love stories but hate a liar. If they even once catch you lying, you will never ever get their confidence. The classic notion of 'You cannot sell if you don't speak a lie' doesn't apply to them.

Never blame anyone

You can't do that, simple, you need to rather think of what would have gone wrong during the call. Successful sales people have always tried thinking what they could have done differently, what could have been prevented, what could have been done rightly. They go back to the drawing board and think again, make notes and practice, they don't blame people, products, company or the circumstances. They take responsibility for their actions and stand by their words.

Know your own worth

Successful sales people are aware of their strength's and weakness, hence they stay within their own limits. They do not require anybody else to confirm their worth. They do not feel the need to come up to somebody's expectations. They are fully aware of their actions as they believe that their actions will bring them the respect they deserve. They value their esteem, freedom and focus on personal growth and are always helping & contributing to the growth of other's around them. Without expecting any return from anyone, hence they are never disappointed with people. They have always good things to say about everyone and are a source of motivation for all. *This is another one that i personally rate high amongst all.*

Never run away from situations / Never believe in shortcuts.

Successful sales people never run away from problems or situations, in fact they take them head on. They do not ignore them but stand up and face them. They know that where they were right or wrong and do not hesitate to confront any situation. They are aware that the longer they let a problem linger, the greater it will become and they will have to face a bigger problem in the future. They believe is early solutions and also get rid of problems as soon as possible.

Move ahead of the Past

Successful sales people do not believe in living in the past, they prefer to learn and move on. They do not waste time on things that have already happened and cannot be reversed. They are quick learners from the past, they learn from the past and quickly move on to focus on the future. They believe in turning their mistakes into learning important lessons and implement them in the times to come. They also do not rest in past laurels and constantly work to create new benchmarks. They know the sales mantra very clearly 'You are as good as your last performance'

Manage time well

'Time is money' and people who believe & respect this are the one's who will always have an edge over others. Successful sales people are aware that time is an extremely critical factor, hence neither waste anybody's time nor theirs. Keeping appointments and respecting the value of other's time is also extremely important. They do not hesitate to politely refuse that cup of tea offered by the retailer if they realize that they are running late as per schedule and believe me that they are respected for that. They are precise, to the point in their communication speaking the right words, addressing the right areas and closing at the earliest. They are well aware that they have a job to do and do not have the whole month to do it.

Be humours

This is one of the most important communication strengths that one can have. Everyone loves a guy with a funny side. Nothing builds a rapport faster than humour, it's a fact. If you can get the other guy to smile or laugh, you got him. Remember not to make any personal jokes as some people may not get it. It is advised that you use personal instances or situations or people faced instead of making them up.

Be a man of character

Stand for things people value honesty, tradition, work ethics, truthfulness, sincerity, dedication, personal habits, language, personal conduct, health etc. Never make loose statements, never talk dirty however friendly you are with the retailer. Everyone loves and admires people with strong moral character. You don't necessarily need to preach one but practice for yourself.

"Stand for something.........
anything" - One of my seniors
told me and i knew that this
was a defining statement.

Chapter 3

Types of a Call

We need to first understand how many types of calls are there, is there any difference

Cold call -

A cold call is when you do not know the customer by any measures or in plain and simple words 'an unsolicited call'. This is not the best way or an effective way to conduct business but many consider it to be quite effective in generating fresh leads and contributing by untraditional ways to business. In this kind of calling it is not even sure that the person or establishment is even a consumer of your product or services. Also You are meeting or calling on him for the first time, without an appointment not knowing if he is the decision maker or he knowing anything about you. He will most probably be shortlisted from different random mediums i.e. telephone book, random database, internet, any particular & specific database, target group, using particular product or services etc. He may not necessarily be the one to buy your product or services but maybe a prospective buyer. Cold calling is mostly done on phone to generate leads but is also done as a warm contact in many organizations to generate fresh business. Cold calls are also conducted for research purposes also apart from selling product & services.

Appointment call

This call is made when everything is prefixed and your client / customer / retailer expects you at a certain fixed time. You have already spoken to him and discussed certain aspects or prospects of business. You are aware of the person his business and his requirements. Moreover he also has an idea of your purpose and knows that you are visiting as he has granted you permission to meet him. Chances of productivity are high in this case as you have already done the preliminary discussions and he is willing to discuss more or know more to what you offer and take the discussions ahead. He is aware of what you are coming for and will be prepared to discuss with you ahead of the basic discussions. You are also well prepared to handle his objections as you are already aware of some of his issues & requirement.

Pitch call

This client is your clear consumer of the products or services that you provide. He is important and can make a difference to your business. You know his needs well or have been already briefed about the requirements. You go and meet him as a team and more than one person is involved as there are different aspects to be addressed. Advertising companies, contract manufacturing etc. fall into this space. These are mostly single large accounts and can give you long term and sizeable business.

Retailer call

This the one of the most important in mom & pop / brick & mortar context as with a base of millions of retail outlets spread across the globe and millions of products, it's the heart of the business and economy in any progressive / developing country as it concerns dealing with the biggest chunk of consumers. This also involves one of the biggest industry which is FMCG (Consumer goods overall) and also has the largest chunk of retail outlets worldwide. This call is generally done mostly on individual retail establishments in the consumer market selling products directly to small & big retailers who in terms sell the products to the end consumer. The retailer is the backbone of traditional consumer products business and an established consumer of your products or services. All kinds of retailers and businesses fall under this category.

Services call

This is a call made to sell intangible products (a service as a product). It is generally done for a business that does work for a customer, and occasionally provides goods, but is not involved in manufacturing. There is no physical product in hand to sell most of the times and all you have is a presentation folder with details of service. The food industry, insurance sector, courier services, yearly maintenance of consumer goods etc. may fall under this.

Referred calling

This call is arisen out of an existing need or a personal effort to connect two possible individuals to explore business opportunities. This call has arisen out of a reference or networking so assume half of the comfort level will already be there. In spite of that you should not expect to make a sale on the first visit itself. The first visit is more of to understand each other than sell or buy anything.

Chapter 4

Customers are People

Understanding the customer

Some sales people have varied notions about retailers and the sales call and believe in a lot of grape wine or market intelligence. Try and put yourself in his shoes, you will get better answers. Understanding your customers most pressing issues, problems and desires yourself first, is extremely important. Each individual has a specific want or need and is naturally receptive to absorbing information that helps meet their challenges & issues. He is an individual like you and runs a small enterprise like you have a job to do.

– His first and foremost intention is to safeguard his business / enterprise interests.

   – His second motive is to make maximum profits.

   – His third motive is to excel in his business and be respected in the society and specially within the business community.

So once we know these facts we should respect them as we would do the same.

Hence, extremely important for everyone is to get the facts right about him. Some universal facts are:

1. Never be mistaken - He is the boss

2. Business comes first to him

3. They are well aware that you have come for business and you mean only that.

4. They clearly understand that you represent an organization and are bound by rules.

5. They will try and squeeze out more from you citing different reasons or techniques (as you will too) but that all is strictly professional.

6. Do not cross the line of professional etiquette however friendly he may seem.

7. He has no intention of being related to you.

8. You can never win by proving him wrong

9. Even if he is sitting ideal, his time is very precious & yours too.

10. They are always looking for more and newer opportunities to do business in spite of the various risks involved.

Understand customer perception

Understanding customer perception is extremely important as knowing who your customers are. This is particularly important as it allows you to adjust to the feedback and compensate for where you fall short. Lack of customer understanding makes it difficult for you to effectively & precisely answer his objections. If you don't answer his query's or objections with satisfaction consider the call & business lost. Customers are less loyal and far less trusting than they used to be and are also much more informed & aware today than they used to be. Today's social media environment has given them the power to research themselves, rethink & evaluate their purchase decisions. So, if you don't understand them how can you possibly deliver the types of experiences they desire?

Customers are human beings

You have to understand first that the retailer is a human being like you. He will hate you love you, respect you for the same reasons that you will do to your friends, colleagues and near and dear one's for. Most of the customers that you come across will be simple human beings, sentimental and emotional and enjoying basic and very small things in life. They have less demands, they are not that fussy, their habits will be simple & uncomplicated, they will mostly have no air about them & will adjust to situations keeping things simple. They enjoy simple things and even celebrate small occasions. They do not look for big opportunity or a big occasion, for them enjoying simple and small things everyday is the way of life. Most of them can be handled with respect and professionalism.

Before making the call you have to understand the circumstances of your customer. You will have to make psychological discoveries so that your call incorporates that

Example: If he has a recent celebration in his family a congratulations is in order. If there has been a sad incident in his family a condolence is in order.

Power of emotions

Emotions are the key drivers behind our everyday decisions specially while dealing with people. Emotions are crucial for building long term relationships with your customers. A focus on building long term bonds is beneficial for any individual throughout his career. A successful sales person always looks to building bonds instead of pushing sales. Emotions can move mountains and it is true for long and short term both.

What cannot be achieved by the grandeur of the organization, your personality, high profitability promises, excellent selling skills or any such strong positing, can be achieved by a strong emotional connect. Customers think both with their rational & emotional brains and you need to handle both for any kind of success. Remember it is emotions on which some of the greatest brands across the world are built.

Important to understand is that we do not overdo it. If you overdo it, it is almost certain that it will not go your way. The whole point will be lost and he will definitely use it for his advantage. You have to maintain a line of professional decorum whatever the case, remember business comes first.

Establish a relationship

Everyone wants to do business with someone they can connect. They want to do business with friends, be a friend, be helpful. I always asked questions about where they come from and how did they get into this or how do they like it in this big city coming from a smaller place or also tried to find something in common to connect and establish a relationship. I always found something and my relationship went beyond 'selling'. This was one big factor which not only made me sail thru but also put me apart from the rest of the bunch and i was always quoted as the 'sales guy with the best market connect' in the country.

I was personal but not too personal, i always maintained the thin line. I always indulged to the limit the retailer / customer wanted me to. I always tested the waters, researched around, asked questions and indulged when i was almost sure. If meeting for the first time i was extremely positive, smiling, to the point, honest & straightforward and that helped me break the ice and put him at ease to talk business which eventually led to a relationship of professional respect which later converted into a personal bond.

Sell to help

It's a totally different philosophy and anyone who believes in this one, will definitely go quite far, in fact all the way is what i strongly believe. A successful sales person is always 'with' the retailer / customer as a friend rather than being only a sales person to get the sales and move. Do not forget he gets hundred's of sales persons trying to persuade him to buy something or the other that he may not wish to buy but he always looks for friends who he can trust to buy and help him buy.

He is very well aware that you know the product better than him, hence will always look towards you for help to make the buying decision and then the re-assurance too. A successful sales guy never believes to 'just make the kill' and move on, in fact he knows that he has an extremely responsible job to do apart from selling his product or service. He has to help him to choose the right product and help him increase his business and profits. In doing so he makes many friends, is loved by all, gains much more respect and is able to excel wherever he works as everyone just loves him.

Chapter 5

Sales call - Why is a Structure Important

Why is a structured sales call Important?
or is it important at all???

So what is a structural approach or rather what is a structure 'A structure is a scientific explanation of the fundamentals on which something has been constructed'. I may not be fully right in my definition but that's what i could construct in order to explain a structure by definition.

Let me again explain you in a more practical way. So you have a cook book which you at times refer for a recipe of any dish. So there are instructions which you follow to reach the desired result. The process will suggest you the best way to get that perfect dish, that's a structure to create a perfect dish. However nowhere is it mentioned in any cookbook that you can't make deviations, you are in the driver's seat and can make little deviations. So you can follow a structure and yet be creative in your approach to get even better or desired results. Finally, the human DNA too has a structure.

More important for us is to realize that it is not about the product, the price, the market or the competition, it's about the person making the call who can make the killing difference. Every word and action taken during a call leads to reactions and objections. Hence to minimize objections and to be more effective & precise, a structure & layered approach is required. The call needs to be controlled in order not to go astray or venture into areas you do not wish to.

Have you ever seen a sculptor use his clay for making a model, his wheel speed has to be right, his mixture has to be of the right consistency, his timing to apply has to be right, his handling has to be delicate and his strokes have to be precise. He has to mould the clay in quick time and gently to get the desired shape. He has to plan for exigencies to correct any mistakes and if need be do it all over again, he will do it again till he achieves a perfect shape.

If you drink too much of water before your meal you may not be able to eat your meal properly. Hence you have to balance both. You need to know what comes first and what is more important.

For example, If you do not introduce yourself properly before the call he might not be comfortable discussing business with a stranger. He needs to know you properly and what you have come for before he starts discussing anything with you. You have to put him at ease to be in a positive frame of mind to discuss business.

Again, if you share the price before sharing the benefits of the product it may seem too expensive and he may not buy. You also need to state the facts with proof and share knowledge for your benefits. The more you educate and share the more he believes you and understands you.

The structure and process is what make the difference between a failed effort & a succesful sales closure. So if you do it knowingly, you will always be in control and achieve desired results. A structured & layered call helps you not only to control the call but also minimize the possible objections. You can be in control all the time & bring him to where you want and close effectively in your favour.

The 7 steps

Lets began.....

Chapter 6

The Seven Steps of an Effective Sales Call

Step 1, Planning & preparation

These arc two simple words but the most important and effective ones. This is the first step for any given product or services to be created or actioned.

It is like preparing a drawing of a house that you want to construct. Leave one simple detail unplanned and you go thru hundreds of unknown problems later. Your entire success depends on these two simple things. Whatever the product or service if you have not planned properly & adequately, your chances of success are already a question mark.

As always said well planned is half done

So where does planning start........

It starts much before the call, it starts at your home. It may also start a day earlier

So you can divide 'Planning & Preparation's' in two parts

1) Before you leave home

2) Once you reach the market.

So if you have far to go, you need to wake up early and have to plan it the night before. Getting up early you need to get dressed early and schedule to leave for work earlier than normal.

If the place you work has less or no arrangement of food, you need to ask your family / wife to make sure that your lunch is packed in time for you to carry it.

You need to make sure that your vehicle has enough fuel otherwise you need to incorporate time to fill in the fuel from your place of choice.

You also need your clothes, shoes etc ironed and ready for you to be on time and you need to plan all that a day earlier.

You need to make sure that your mobile or tab is fully charged for the day.

Your alarm clock working to make sure you rise in time to go to that market far away, as you need extra time to reach far off places.

So you see how early can the planning and preparation can began. Isn't it much earlier than you thought it to be, surprised you are as you never thought that way.

Having taken care of all that you need to look into several other aspects before you leave home

1. Is your work bag ready

2. Are your visiting cards in your pocket

3. Are your market details ready

4. Is your customer database / details for today ready

5. Do you need to reconfirm your appointments before you leave

6. Do you have enough cash in your wallet for the day.

7. Are your tools to be used during the call ready

8. Do you have you route call plan ready

9. Do you have records of previous calls of that route ready

Make a checklist of things that need to be done daily or stuff you need to carry daily along with you and tick it every day before leaving.

So now with part one done, you are ready to leave for the market. Once you have reached the market, you now move to the second part of planning and preparation. Now in order to make your day most productive you need to plan the below.

1. Find a proper parking place for your vehicle so that you do not have to worry about that the whole day or for the couple of calls that you need to make in that area.

2. Determining which will be your first call as the decision maker might leave if you follow the set route.

3. You may need to reorganize your bag, take out the sales call folder or tab and keep it ready.

4. Log in to your work site in your mobile tab if you use one for a call & attendance.

5. Comb your hair or wash your face again if required, tuck in your shirt and if need be wipe your shoes.

6. Take out your detailer / order book in order to make the call, take out your pen and keep it handy. Fill up the details (Name, market, date, today's target etc.) and get ready.

Is there anything left to do? Yes one last check of the ammunition needed for the call

Check your bag

Check your SALES presenter / folder / builder

Check your retailer record card (DRCP, if you have them)

Check your pen and other tools

Check your product samples

Wipe of the sweat, make yourself look fresh.

Spray some deodorant (If required as you definitely don't want to smell bad).

Spit that chewing gum or any other substance in your mouth and if need be rinse it.

Sales presenter / Folder / Builder

The most important & extremely powerful tool that any sales person can gave, make sure that it is always with you, updated and in top condition. It should contain all the information required to make the call i.e. products details, features & benefits, offers and media & BTL plan. It generates curiosity, brings the attention & interest and you can create a lot of excitement with it. Any great organization worth its value spends a great deal and pays utmost importance to this particular tool. You can also put your DSR at the end of it. Re-adjust the sequence of the sales presenter / folder / builder (As per the need of the call) and it suggested to be as follows.

1. Place All Products one by one (One page for one product or range), never put 2-3 products on the same page (Ideally) (Different sizes in same range can be shown).

2. Focus products or the ones which you want to sell first should be the ones in the first pages, start the call with them always.

3. Relevant offers to be mentioned with relevant products.

4. ATL plan sheets followed by BTL plan sheets

5. Merchandising material samples (POS).

6. One page on some local or company highlights.

7. DSR at the end.

Using the sales presenter / folder / builder properly is also extremely important. Couple of points on how to use your sales presenter / folder / builder.

1. Always point the display pages towards the retailer.

2. Go one product at a time, even if your customer / retailer wants to rush thru. Politely request him to wait till you reach his desired product.

3. Use a pointer (Pen) to focus on important points, it always helps bring focus and attention.

4. Never give / handover you product detailer / presenter to the retailer, remember that it is your weapon, so do not give it in somebody else's hands.

5. Respect the sales presenter / folder / builder keep it well maintained.

6. Make sure it has everything needed to make the call as it also reminds you of any points you may miss.

Having taken care of all that you are now ready for your first call. Go ahead with confidence as you have prepared well and taken care of the most important aspect of the call.

Step 2, Observation

So, what is so great about something like 'Observation' that we need to make this as an important step in the sales call.

Extremely important, as this forms an integral & important part of your call and helps you take decisive actions. It lets you make important discoveries which you will need as tools to be used during the call. Observation gives you the ammunition to win the battle.

Observation leads to great understanding if your are paying attention.

Observation can create powerful insights and may reveal the quite obvious things that you may miss.

Observation let's you make that last minutes micro changes.

So, where does the observation start?

It starts once you start walking towards the retailer and can be classified into two sections, 1) before you reach the outlet, 2) after you reach the outlet.

Observations before you reach the customer / retailer / outlet

It starts right from the time you decide to make a call to a certain retailer.

You have to observe from a distance if the shop you have to call is open.

You have to observe from a distance if he is all set for business or is still setting up.

You have to observe from a distance if the key person is available or not.

You have to observe from a distance if already another sales person is making a call.

You need to observe if there are customers already in the outlet and the key person is busy.

You have to observe walking towards the retailer what is the name of his shop.

You have to observe from a distance if the retailers name is also mentioned on the board and note it down.

Observations once you reach the outlet

You have to observe if you can see your products somewhere in the shop.

You have to observe if available what all products does he have of your company.

You have to observe what competition he is selling.

You have to observe and guess the quantity and range of your products, this will help you close the call.

You need to observe where to merchandise your products after the call.

What kind of merchandising resource and where it is available in the shop.

Look for clues, ideas to merchandise, beautiful displays.

Look for trophies, pictures, awards or any decoration which you can use during the call.

You will need every bit of information during your call.

But is observation limited to you only...........absolutely not, the retailer also makes his own observations and we need to be aware of that. So what does he observe?

Rule of the 4 x 20's

First 20 steps

That is the distance from where he starts noticing / seeing you. Hence your first 20 steps have to be well put forward. They should be confident, balanced and steady. Once he see's a confident well dressed man approaching towards his shop, he also starts to gets ready to face him. He starts to notice your personality, dressing, walk and forms the first impression about you. He draws an idea of you and your personality.

First 20 inches

Extremely important as that's what he can see of you (from behind his counter) and form the first opinion about you. If he sees a person panting, with sweat all over, untidy shirt struggling with himself, you are already done and have lost the first impression. Your first 20 inches have to be impeccable, neat face, combed hair, spotless shirt, neat tie and looking fresh. If your customer see's a delightful smiling, and smart looking guy he is already ready to discuss with such a person.

First 20 seconds

Your first 20 seconds are what matter the most. In fact to say that a positive atmosphere to buy develops here would not be wrong. From the moment you reach his shop shake that hand, have a great smiling face and say something, you have received a first 'yes' to the call and created an atmosphere which is positive and favourable for you. You have to be your best in the first 20 seconds.

First 20 words

Finally the first 20 words that you say matter the most. He has observed you and he is already almost certain that you are here for business and most probably to sell him something. What you say to first or to start with has to put him at ease, otherwise your call is lost. All the suspicions that he may have about you have to end with the first 20 beautiful words that release the pressure & breaks the ice.

So now you also experience how important a simple thing as observation can be as it will help you get that first line right. The power of observation is immense and can be felt during the call. Observation will help you avoid unnecessary discussions, kill many possible objections and help determine the products and quantity for your closing of the call.

Step 3, Introduction

*Why is introduction so important or is a
proper introduction even necessary?*

The questions that you should ask yourself before
answering the above question is:

How will someone know who i am?

How will someone know what do i do?

How will someone know for what i have come for?

How will someone react to a newcomer to his
establishment?

How will he respect me?

Will he actually be ready to discuss business?

The answer is only one 'You need to introduce yourself
properly' to remove these questions from his mind. A
proper introduction will put him at ease and also create
a favourable and positive atmosphere for discussions.

So how do you introduce yourself?

First - Greetings, Good morning, Good afternoon, Good evening, Hello, (Using local language an intellect is a great thing it helps in making him comfortable).

Second - Client / Retailer name first - Mr. Ram Gupta (Ideally the full name) but if it is not known, the surname or maiden name will do.

Third - Your name - Always introduce yourself by your full name.

Fourth - Organization name - Always mention your organization name in full (Ideally).

Fifth - Purpose - State your purpose of visit

Sixth - And the most important - Make a positive statement to start the conversation in a positive & favourable atmosphere.

Seventh - Always ask for his time, even if he is doing nothing, It makes him feel important.

Do this every time you meet him and are making the call. This not only makes him feel good, makes him comfortable but also makes him attentive for the call. He too needs some moments to recall and prepare for the call and discussion. A proper introduction helps him get the connect and pick it up from where he was last time or ready him for any conversation.

So let's now construct the entire introduction

Good morning Mr. Ram Gupta, I am Rajiv Sharma from R.C. Industries and would request couple of minutes of your precious time to present.

For Trainers

Please practice the greetings with each individual in the group. If the group is too large please ask them to make pairs and do it with each other.

Step 4, Opening the call

Having introduced yourself, you now need to make the opening statement which not only complements the purpose but also sets a positive tone for the call. Remember first 20 words, you can't falter here, you have done all the right things now you just have to say something which eases you into the call and at the same time puts the customer / retailer at ease.

Remember about the advertisement commercial which has only thirty seconds to tell a story, explain the product & make an impact so powerful that the consumer is compelled to buy.

So what will be an exciting first sentence to start with?

How are you?

How is the business?

Weather seems great?

Would you like to buy products from my company

See my products first, i will leave quickly

Some don't even make any opening statement and just say their company name (As if they are the last word for that kind of products) and hand over the product detailer to the retailer to see for himself.

Let us analyze some of them

How are you? - This is probably the worst one to start with. Is he ever good, especially if he realizes that you have come to sell him something.

How is the business? - Is the business ever good, It is never good as he is not sure of the purpose of anyone asking that. Why is he asking this, does he mean that i make good money or not, maybe he gets me caught into tax problems, maybe he will have to buy something from you if he say's that the business is good. In my 25 years of sales career i have never heard any retailer saying 'Yes' business is booming, even if he has grown from a mom & pop store to a huge supermarket.

Weather seems great? - Yeah you think so? i don't like this weather at all.

So what do you say that puts him in a positive frame of mind and he is open to listen to you.

Now consider couple of facts

1. Everyone likes self praise (Great looks, Unique hair style, branded clothes etc.)

2) Everyone likes to be talked about anything him/her has a contribution / association in community and takes pride in (Instrumental in cleaning his lane, winning local elections, being appointed a member of a prestigious body)

3. Everyone like to be greeted on any achievement by any member of his family (Achievement in sports, academics, politics, Job, new vehicle etc.)

4. Everyone likes to be greeted on special occasions in his family (Wedding, Birthday, Anniversary, New born, opening of another business)

5. Everyone likes to listen to anything unique achieved by him / her.

6. Everyone loves to talk about all things / causes he / she cares about

Remember the objective is to set up a positive atmosphere and find a subject or an idea that is of mutual interest.

What we need to avoid

1. Religious subjects

2. Political subjects

3. Topics which are controversial

4. Incidents which are sensitive

5. Any personal strong statements

You can also say something which immediately creates excitement, cuorisity or is of great interest to him.

− I have excellent news for you on the products you were looking for.

− I have some exciting & never before promotions for you.

− I am here to introduce an exciting new line of products which you have been waiting for.

− I have come to you with excellent news for you, you have won the contest, congratulations.

− Mr. Ram you look fabulous in this attire, i admire your dressing sense.

− Let me first tell you that your shop is one of the best organized and clean from the entire market that i visit, credit to you.

− Let me first congratulate you on the birth of your child, trust the mother & child are doing well.

You have to start with a statement that brings an agreement and makes him smile, you are in. Establishing a positive atmosphere for the call is the first 'Yes' that you get. Your half the work is done if the call starts on a strong positive feeling, he is already to buy.

So now we are back to our original question 'what do we say to start with'. We may say something like this:

If you are going for the first time or have met him only twice or thrice

Good morning Mr. Ram Gupta, I am Rajiv Sharma from R.C. Industries and request 10 minutes from you to share my product details

Namaskar Ram ji, I am Rajiv Sharma from R.C. Industries and i have an excellent promotional offer for you, can you spare five minutes please

Good morning Mr. Ram Gupta, I am Rajiv Sharma from R.C. Industries, i see an excellent display of our products and want to congratulate you on that.

Good morning Mr. Ram Gupta, I am Rajiv Sharma from R.C. Industries, i must say that your shop is one of the most organized and neat one i have ever seen, i see a lot of personal efforts.

Remember, don't try to be too friendly that too in the first couple of visits, this may offend him or make him suspicious.

If you already know him well

Good morning Mr. Ram Gupta, I am Rajiv Sharma from R.C. Industries i am here today to share a great news and will just take five minutes of yours.

Hello / Good morning Gupta ji, how wonderful it is to see you in that white shirt, you look great!............ Can i take five minutes of yours to share the new exciting promotions.

Good afternoon Gupta ji and congratulations on your son topping the college, you would be very proud

Namaskar Ram ji, my first stop is always at your shop as i get inspired to see you so energetic always!

If during the observation you have noticed that the retailer in a gloomy mood or in a serious mood, be polite & ask. Be sensitive to his issues and leave if you come to know there is something serious that has happened. Do not forget to apologize and leave immediately. You definitely do not want to make the call in such circumstances. He will always remember this gesture of yours. Remember 'Customers are people'.

Know what you 'actually' sell

You also need to make impactful statements which are powerful enough to make the other guy say 'Wow'. You need to exactly understand what you say with words and what you actually mean by that. You need to be absolutely clear what do you 'exactly or actually' sell. Just for your understanding you sell benefits and usefulness arisen out of the product or services and not what you physically have. For this you need to be creative and innovative and find out the exact words to say that. This is what will stand you out from the hundreds of sales persons that he meets in a day or thousands he meets in his life.

A car salesman - Doesn't sell cars he is selling pride and status

A shaving products salesman - He doesn't sell blades and razors he sells grooming.

A insurance salesman - He doesn't sell insurance he sells financial protection to one's own family.

A clothes salesman - He doesn't sell clothes he sells style and fashion.

Be very aware of what business you actually are in to make impactful statements.

So, to sum it up the whole idea of the introduction is to create a favourable and positive atmosphere for the call to start on a strong & positive note.

For Trainers

Now you should practice the opening sentence with the group. Involve them in the discussions and interesting things will be revealed. Ask them to role play and greet each other. List down the best introductions and offer chocolates to the best suggestions (Keep them handy for instant rewards). Keep the charts & markers handy.

Step 5, Presentation

So now having reached the retailer, done the introduction, said those magical first words, now is the time for the real thing. Making a presentation is like handling an orchestra and even if one instrument or one musician is not aligned and controlled the entire music will go for a toss.

What is the definition of presentation?

'To clearly, consciously & effectively communicate about your product & services to your possible customer'

Your presentation should bring out the below mentioned three things:

— *An opportunity for the retailer to save something*

— *An opportunity to increase or add something*

— *An opportunity to solve something*

The call has to be well orchestrated and everything required for that has to be ready & handy with you at all times. The presentation folder ready, samples ready, pointer (if using) ready, your assistant (if you have) should be on to your right hand side ready to take the cue and hand over the samples or anything required as soon as he gets the cue.

The major tools required for a call are:

1. Product detailer / Presentation in tab (if you use one)

2. Product samples (Specially new products, Promotional products, New MRP or pack changes etc.)

3. A pointer

4. Daily report pad or dealer card

5. Tablet (if you work with one)

6. Order book

7. New POS (Point of sale) material

8. Merchandising kit (Scissors, tape, board pins, nails, hammer (optional))

Why all that? is all that really important?

Well if you are going for a war, you might as well carry the pistols, guns, armour, helmets etc. otherwise you may be shot dead from far and all that skill and training would be of no use.

Brief notes on each material / tool that has been suggested above.

Product detailer should have all the range properly arranged. You should always change the sequence of the products as per your needs and priority. The detailer is important so that not only your sequence of presenting the products is right but also you can control the flow. It will also help you to not forget any product from the entire range. Also a presentation folder communicates a 'Factual' factor, it means if it is written it might be true. It has to be in pristine condition and without any extra papers etc.

The samples have to go with the product that you are talking about, one at a time. If he see's too many products he will get distracted and confused and the focus will be lost. The beauty of making the call is to be in control at all times and take him where you want. If someone is assisting you he needs to be on your right side ready with the sample that you may need. He has to work in tandem with you and should know what to show and when. Why on the right side because it will be easy for you to take the sample and give back to him (if you are a right hander). Again the samples have to be in excellent condition as they represent the products that will reach the retailer, change them daily if required.

New product samples, pack changed, consumer offer product samples are surely important but never forget that bread and butter generic product that has made your company or comprises of the bulk of your business. Do not take your brands / products for granted as some people prefer not carrying samples. That clearly shows not only his arrogance but also that he has no intentions of finding new customers or opening that crucial new outlet. A sample being carried is equal to an advertisement running and remind everyone who see's it about the product.

Why is a pointer needed? well it brings focus to what & where you want him to see or read. You could use a pen too and it will bring the required focus to your call. Research says that more attention is paid if you point towards something.

A dealer card or any type of document to record the retailer customer details, purchase records, previous purchases is desired and quite beneficial tool. You have ready reference to the previous purchases, buying pattern, previous issues, pending issues, previous quantities etc. will help you a lot in determining product & quantities.

An order book (Ideally) is required as you need to write down the order and any other remark that you wish to write. You will not remember everything and will not want to miss any important comment on which you need to get back to the retailer or need to send him something. That small note is as important as anything. Always make sure that you make note of small things, promises, commitments etc. the retailer will immensely appreciate these small gestures and will always remember it.

POS material (Point of sale) is a salient sales man for every product. So if you don't merchandise after the call, you can be sure of lesser off take. Make sure to carry some POS material for each call and put if after you finish. Successful sales people develop their own material if not provided by the company. There are many options to do that and you can be as innovative as possible, It all depends on you.

Being all set, let's get back to discussing the presentation part in details.

You are now ready for presenting the products, look into his eyes (Don't stare), be confident be relaxed.

Begin by the detailer facing the retailer so that he has a full view and your pointer on what you want him to focus on

Never handover the detailer to him. It's like handing over the advantage to him. Many people give the detailer to the retailer and ask him to see what he wants. Gentlemen, the call is lost, he will straightaway go to what he wants and you will never be able to sell what you want.

Be brief. Be precise. Be clear

Presenting to the decision maker, always.

First things first, always make sure that you are addressing the decision maker

Many people make this cardinal mistake of not making sure that they are presenting to the right person. Only after they have spend all their energies on an excellent presentation they are introduced to the fact that 'i am not the right person to take this decision, please come later as only he can take the call of buying your product / services and that is extremely painful. Please make sure that you meet the right person 'The decision maker'.

Remember the whole purpose of the call is to sell first what you want, along with what he wants.

One product at a time

Always present one product at a time, do not jump. If the retailer wants to jump to something that he is interested in request him to wait till you reach there. If you jump to where he wants to go you lose your focus and end up serving his interests. Sales people using a single sheet or a four page detailer can use a poster to conceal the other products.

Present when you have his full attention

Always make sure that you have his full attention. Never present if he is in the middle of something, wait. Even if he asks you to go on, tell him you can wait. If he insists that he is going to be busy for a while, tell him you will come again. Politely tell him that you are in no hurry and the presentation needs his full attention. It is extremely important that you present with his full attention to you otherwise be rest assured of a refusal or unproductive call due to not understanding your presentation fully.

Never down the competition or name it constantly

It's a no win and doesn't stand you in good books. Talk about your own strengths, USP's, features and benefits rather than criticizing the competition. Also never keep naming the competition, you are advertising it unknowingly. The more you name your competition and list it's features against yours, the more you are creating a recall of your competition. I always mentioned it as 'the competition' or other similar products in the market and just stuck to my product features and benefits.

Don't preach ethics

Always avoid preaching ethics or explaining how ethical you are. Your ethics will show during your call or in your dealing / handling of the retailer. Just be honest, straightforward, truthful and be helpful to him he will know your character. There is a very thin line between self praise and preaching ethics and most of the times salespersons do not know when they have breached it.

Features & Benefits

So how do you make sure that you will sell what you want? for that it is important to understand what actually makes a product sell. What are the different points involved

Features of a product

Benefits of a products

USP of the product

Price of the product

Value for money to the consumer

Now we need to probe a little, what do features of a product do, they tell you about what the product can do........ right?

Wrong...............

Features are important as they lead to benefits of that products, leading to the price seeming less and ultimately value for money to the consumer.

So if you are able to link features to benefits, you have almost sold the product. Always define the features to the benefits leading to value for his money spent. So always features first & then explain the benefits.

See diagram for yourself (For trainers)

Cut out two equal proportion cards as shown. Write 'Features' in the middle of one card and write 'Benefits' in the middle of another card.

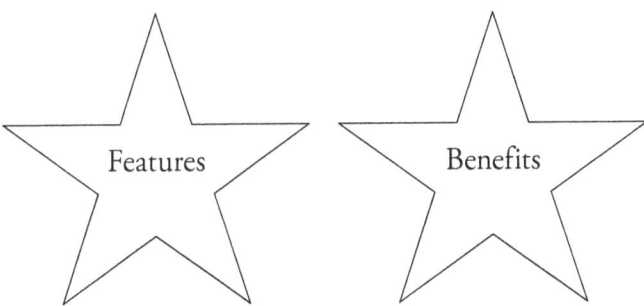

Show both the cards one by one, you will see that the one with 'Benefits' if shown before features will seem smaller and if features card is shown first benefits will seem larger. Try this and you will be surprised.

USP meaning 'Unique selling preposition' of the product is what differentiates your product from the others / competitors and comes next, as that is something which is exclusive only to the company you present. Once you have stated the features and linked them to the benefits that the consumer will enjoy by buying this product, it is time that you highlight the USP of the product as it will add to the attraction and then is when the consumer will compare and derive value to the purchase.

Now if you still do not see a response from the customer, there is definitely something missing from your presentation that you had to address. So how do you know that and what is he thinking about. Sometimes he might say that and that makes it easy for you to address it but what if he keeps silent & is constantly thinking and does not say a word? difficult for you to find out isn't it?

It's now time to make discoveries.

Technical discovery

Check surroundings - Is renovation happening, are there customers waiting, is lunch waiting, is it time to close the outlet.

Check product placements & quantities - If he is over stocked with competition or your products

Check displays - Nobody has merchandised and there are damages

Previous issues - No one attended to his issues for the past two visits.

Psychological discovery

How do you do that? by asking specific questions

Product response - How do you feel about the features, are they not brilliant and unique

Promotion response - Isn't this a great promotion with this kind of a product

Price response - Isn't this the right price given the features?

Customer response - I am sure many of your customers would like to have this.

As soon as he picks one of the above to respond, you know what you have to say.

Personal discovery

Ask if he seems worried about something.

Is there a situation going on in the outlet.

Does he want to leave for some urgent work.

Never forget that you need to be very polite for making any discovery. Anything asked in the slightest of a harsh tone may upset him.

Having said all that we now really need to understand as to what are the reasons that any retailer / customer around the world would buy. Lets jot down a few reasons:

Great Consumer demand

Great Profit

Good credit terms

Great promotion

Popular brand / product

Convenience

Fast selling

Current favourite

Will fetch him pride

Will impress his customers / neighbours / friends

Good quality

Competition doesn't have it

Supplier is a friend

You are a friend

People buy for their own reasons and not yours and they may have many varied reasons to buy. Your job is to listen to them, understand and find the one. Their needs may also point towards their urgency / eagerness to buy.

For Trainers - Do a simple exercise

Now let's do a little exercise with the participants, go to the board / sheets and ask them to list reasons for any retailer buying any product. Ask everyone to give 3 reasons, remove the common ones and write down all the other's. You have a list, now start discussing them one by one, you will get some more common ground and finally you can tell them that any retailer in the world buys mostly for 3 major reasons. I present to you the golden rule of SPQ.

There are primary only three reasons because of which any retailer buy's any product

The Golden rule of

S P Q

Saleability

The first reason because of which any retailer buys a product is saleability as his first & foremost concern is if what he buys will sell off or not. This means products that are fast & easily selling are his first choice. This also means that even if these products give him less profits, he will still keep them as they sell fast and he can rotate his investments and increase his profits.

Profitability

This is the second reason because of which most retailers will buy a product. The products that he makes good profits on are his second choice. It also means that even if these products give him less turnover or do not sell that fast, he will still keep them as they give him good profits and contribute highly to his overall profit.

Quality

That's the third reason because of which any retailer buys a product. This gives his store a certain image for his consumers. He can attract quality consumers by selling quality products. They may not be as profitable as others or they may not give him a faster rotation by selling fast but they definitely give him image. He is able to display them prominently and he takes pride in selling them.

Now you can list down many more reasons (as done above) and then debate it amongst any group, you will see that all the reasons in one form or the other lead to these three basic reasons. The permutations, combinations and sequence can be different based on product to product or retailer type to retailer type but the golden rule stands.

Coming back to the call, the major reason why i have shared the golden rule and explained is that if you do not understand or find out which one of the three is the retailer looking for, your sales cannot happen.

Imagine, he is looking for fast selling (saleable) products and you keep on impressing upon the qualities of your product, will he buy? never

Or he is looking quality products and you keep on explaining about the profitability of the products, will he but? never is the answer again

He is looking for profitable products or fast moving products and you keep on explaining that your products are of high quality, will he buy? the answer will always will be a big NO.

A successful sales person is the one who finds out that which one of these is the retailers actual concern and then hits on that particular point and he will win the battle. The retailer only wants to have an answer on his major concerns and if you just answer that in a satisfying manner your call is done.

For Trainers

Now once you are thru explaining the above you can see that each reason that they mentioned eventually points towards one of the three reasons mentioned above.

Mastering the understanding of buying motives takes time. It is only after thousands of calls and some years that you start picking up the 'Real' motives. Keep asking questions, keep noting down the answers and analyze once you return home, you will start understanding. You questions must be intelligent, they must be different to what others normally ask. I always preferred to ask questions wrapped in asking advice / opinion seeking format, it always helped and the retailer was happy to answer.

When do we reveal the price?

Extremely important question and a very sensitive one too. If you don't mention the price at the right moment all may be lost. So when do we talk about the price?

We talk about it as soon as we have finished relating product features to benefits.

We can also talk about it as soon as we share the promotion on it relating the promotion to benefits.

Remember that price will only look small once you are able to establish the benefits. This is true both for the retailer & the consumer, that is how the retailer will also sell it to the consumer.

Example

So you see gupta ji same product same price with 20% extra inside

Look at the features of the product, the price is nothing compared to it

Some golden rules of stating the price

The don'ts

Never reveal or discuss the price before stating the benefits

Never pause after stating the price, continue with the presentation

Never use words like 'Expensive' you can use competitive or little premium instead

Never use words like 'Cheap' for the cost, instead use 'economical'

The do's

You can sandwich price between related benefits

You can let the retailer also handle or suggest the same (Specially in new products launch). For example what do you think should be the price with these benefits and features.

Minimise the price by using appropriate words. For example say for all these features and benefits the price is just this. Or at this price this is excellent value for money.

You can also make appropriate comparisons with competition if you see a clear advantage. For example sir it costs less than our nearest competitor with many added benefits.

A selling benefit must have a structure

All features in any product lead to some or the other benefit, hence once you present the features, you need make sure that you connect every possible feature to a benefit. Once the retailer sees the product in this light, the costs will also seem less. So whenever he compares it to the benefits, the greater the benefits the lesser the cost seems. This all has to be structured in a such a way that one thing leads to the other and finally the retailer sees a value for money product, which he can easily sell to his customers.

So to simplify everything if i put the entire discussion into a structure and present, it would be as under.

So to understand this clearly let us have a closer look at the Product Feature - Benefit sequence chart

The Product Feature-Benefit sequence chart

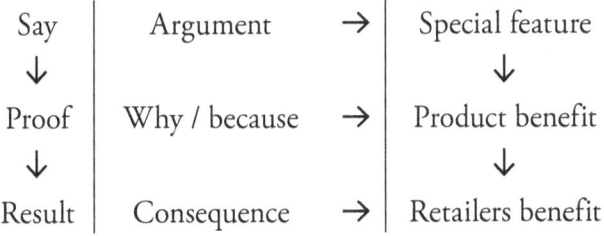

Say	Argument	→	Special feature
↓			↓
Proof	Why / because	→	Product benefit
↓			↓
Result	Consequence	→	Retailers benefit

So now in order to understand the above chart you need to understand the process first.

Column first

Let us go to the first column, so say something (Make a statement or claim) then show the proof and as a consequence it results in a retailer benefit and you close the call productively

Secondly you say something (Make a statement or claim) then show the proof and he raises an objection / questions on the proof, you then take him to the product benefits which translates into the retailer benefits resulting in the call being productive.

Column second

So there is an argument (discussion/ debate) on what you said. You immediately go to the special feature (USP) of the product, which leads to a product benefit (either for the retailer or consumer) which in term translates into a retailer benefit resulting in a productive close. Similarly you can relate how a why because sequence can pan out.

Column Third

Here i have mentioned a rule of thumb, a product feature (USP / Special feature) has to related to a benefit (Either of the retailer or the consumer) which ultimately will lead to a retailer benefit.

So now it all boils down to how efficient and knowledgeable you are to connect the three dots so that the retailer see's a benefit thru features of the product and ultimately result in a productive close for you.

Now for this you have to involve the retailer and he should participate. Ask questions, keep obtaining an agreement from him on each benefit and keep moving till you reach where you want to.

For Trainers

You can now practice this with the group by asking them to list the USP / Features of the products linking them to the benefits and untimely resulting into a retailer or consumer benefit, resulting in a productive close as mentioned earlier.

Once again remember, each feature leads to a benefit and each benefit either lowers the price perception or solves some problem of the consumer or retailer creating a positive and favourable atmosphere for the sale to happen.

Step 6, Objection handling

So objections are a terrible thing, aren't they.......

Correct yourself............In fact the actual sale only starts as soon as the objection is raised.

Objections are not only an integral & important part of the selling process but in fact are an excellent opportunity to understand the retailer's thoughts and what his actual question is. They are in-fact an excellent opportunity to understand what he wants or is looking for.

Another important thing, if they don't object during the conversation or after they've heard you out, either they are not listening or they are not the decision maker / target customer, simple they won't buy.

Never avoid objections. in fact welcome them as they will help you close easily.

Objections in fact are a gateway to his inner thoughts and once the gateway is open you can refer to the golden rule of SPQ and hit the nail on its head. It's their way of wanting to know more. Most objections are sincere one's stemming out of their ignorance or curiosity or incomplete information with him.

The fact is that the retailer exactly knows what he wants and makes sure that he communicates it to us but many a times we are so self obsessed by ourselves, our product, our company or other things that we fail to understand his communication / signals or totally ignore it. So please pay attention and listen to him very carefully.....

Some extremely important things that you need to remember before handling objections:

Be a good listener

The biggest and the most important trait of a sales person is to be a good listener. Most of the times what is said initially is what is foremost that he wants to know. If you don't listen properly and miss it, you might keep guessing for the rest of the call to find out what he exactly wants. Just 'Shut up' every time he speaks and listen to him fully and patiently, never interrupt, never. Listen to the words carefully, listen to the tone and look into his eyes, get the words and actions fully.

Don't listen to answer, listen to understand, make a note of this.

Speak the truth, always

Why tell a lie, as a lie is short lived and most certainly will never carry far. Never tell them a lie for whatever reason as in all probability he may already know the truth. Sometimes they just want to see if you are able to say it or have the courage to mention it. Even if they do not know, if they discover that you lied to them, you have lost the customer forever. Everyone wants a ethical sales person to deal with so be honest, be truthful never tell a lie. The retailer always wants to be treated honestly, do that.

Never sell, Help him buy

This is a big one and i always rated it higher than any of the other one's i mentioned. He is there to buy products as that's what he makes his living selling. He is also willing to deal with you as it is an essential part of his business, all he wants from a salesman is to help him buy, so don't cheat him or take him for granted. He will even blindly trust you if you are able to establish a connect and get his faith but if you trick him that's the end of your relationship and any further dealings. He will always remember and trust a person who has not come to only sell but to help him buy. A sales call is all about helping him to make a decision to buy...........make a note somewhere.

Never ever argue

That's one thing which you need to learn and practice, never argue even if it is evident that the retailer is wrong or is ignorant of the facts. This is the worst thing that any sales person can do. Remember no one is wrong, there are only different point of views. The most important question that you need to ask is 'What do i gain by proving him wrong', absolutely nothing is the answer, in fact you are the biggest loser.

'You never win any customer or argument by proving him wrong' get that straight. You are there out to win friends, not arguments.

We first need to know what causes objections or why objection occur. Some common reasons are

- Poor presentation

- You have not established the need

- You have not been able to establish rapport

- You have not established trust or credibility

- Poor call structure

- Lack of product knowledge

- Poor reading of situation or circumstances

- Personal reasons (Personal hygiene, poor appearance, poor manners, wrong attitude)

- Poor / wrong timing

We also need to know the various forms of objections

- Questions on product quality & company standing

- Criticism of products & company

- Complaints

- Sarcasm

- Showing busy

- Avoiding conversation

- Avoiding eye contact

What are the immediate measures / actions that you need to take as soon as there is an objection raised

Be patient

Show interest & concern in his objection

Listen to him fully till he has finished

Never interrupt

Watch his actions carefully

Do not jump to conclusions

Make mental notes of points to answer later

Be calm and composed

Hold your temper, be polite

Fact of the matter is that there are no new objections, you have heard them all before

Now how do you handle objections, what are the rules, are there any?

First things first, you never win an argument by proving him wrong, even if he is. Even if you are right about pointing about something he has stated, which may not be true or right, you need to do it politely & softly. You cannot hurt his ego, pride, status, knowledge level and win it. Any kind of argument should be a strict no no.

Secondly never bluntly tell him that he is wrong, even if he is, you have to put it across in a suggestive way so that it seems like a suggestion or a point of view. Never use words like 'you are wrong' or 'you don't understand' or 'You don't know' instead you may say 'Maybe i suggest another point of view' or 'Let us look at it this way'.

You have to hear him fully and understand if his objection stems from lack of knowledge about the product or subject, try and share knowledge about the product or in general (Maybe you have missed something during the presentation, go back to the presentation). His ignorance of the matter may also be due to his upbringing, circumstances, education level or nature of business. You have to suggest or show him the less travelled path for him and he will only respect you.

Finally if he is right about something, agree to it without any hesitation. In fact you should thank him for the knowledge shared, he will be pleased. You can even appreciate him for his knowledge on the subject or teaching you something new as may be the case.

The fact is that most objections are born from your presentation itself, so be very precise in what you say & present.

It is also important that you need to show interest in his objections. He should feel that his objection is of importance to you too and you are keen to answer his objections and solve his queries. It also gives him a feeling or sense of achievement, that he is able to make a point.

Objections can broadly classified into two categories

Genuine (That is a proof of interest)

Excuse / stall (Has originated out of self defence)

You need to listen to him very carefully & find out which one of the above two it is and plan and act accordingly.

I will now share with you some techniques on objection handling that you should be using depending on the situation.

Objections can be simple to handle with if you practice the below mention simple things

1. Have excellent product knowledge

2. Have s positive attitude

3. You are willing to listen

4. You have proper and detailed knowledge of your customer

5. You are creative and innovative

6. You seem honestly willing to help

7. Your persistence

Techniques of objection handling

Yes there are techniques that help in objection handling and applying them with a bit of intelligence will produce fabulous results. I am sharing with you some of the most important ones.

The 'Yes but' technique

So now he has made an objection which might not be true. You now have to bring him to a point where he sees a point of view and is in a situation to agree. So what is the technique, say as below

You are correct......but

Yes I agree with you......but

Yes It is possible.......but

Yes It might be a very good idea.......but

The whole idea of the technique is to seemingly agree to what he has said but present your point of view. He will not feel offended and will most probably take it as an advice as you know the best about your product & services.

Based on the need, go back to the presentation and start all over again on the product or feature or benefits as the case may be, you may have missed something.

Probing / digging technique

This particular technique is used when you have not fully been able to understand his objection or he is not able to exactly state the objection. Ask him further

Apart from that do you feel......

OK, Let's assume this.......

Suppose that this is this way..........

Can i hear more about this......

Do you mean to say that........

Listen to what he says, find out what you may have missed during presentation. Go back to the product detailer and start all over again.

The boomerang technique

This technique is used when you find the objection touching something which is important for him to understand. You send the objection straight back to him in the form of an opportunity

It is exactly for the reason...........

Keeping the same thing in mind only

It is exactly as you say

Basically this technique is all about 'Answering a question with a question'. You will see that he will find the answer to his query in the same. Go back to the product detailer and start all over again.

Overriding technique

This is to convert a genuine statement into an opportunity which you can clearly foresee. He may not have see or evaluated in that manner but if you show him the path he may follow.

I don't sell this.........

This is a new category.......

I have never thought about this product or service.............

This is precisely the reason i am presenting you the same, it's an excellent opportunity for you and you must try this out. Go back to the product detailer and start all over again.

Couple of important suggestions

Show interest in his objections

Agree on minor points

Never interrupt

Minimise discussions

Answer briefly

Do not waste too much time

Do not answer every objection

Never make statement or false promises to cover up or accommodate a genuine issue of the retailer.

If he has a valid suggestion, make a note & do not forget to thank him.

Remember you have an important task to do "Close the sale as quickly as possible"

Step 7, Closing the call

This is the most crucial & important part of the sales call. You can say that the sales call is all about closing the sales efficiently in the least possible time. I have seen many sales people making amazing calls but not able to close effectively & productively, it's a total waste.

There are full blown books only on sales closing discussing everything from ways and means to numerous techniques, behaviour, mannerisms, etc. and then it is endless. It is the most tricky part and needs all the skill, smartness and training that one can have. It's a skill easily mastered by the 'street smart' as it requires a lot of logic, anticipation, foresight & wit.

All kinds of fancy literatures and tips are available in the market and i have gone through so many of them. Believe me they are a waste of time money and energy. Most of them talk about things which are very general but are more jargons and flaunting then the real thing. What i present to you has been practiced by thousands of sales persons quite successfully over many years. Moreover it is quite relevant and simple in the overall holistic context.

The definition

Closing is all about getting someone to take a decisive action. Imagine being pressured into doing something you do not wish to do. It is human nature to resist the very thought of being pressured into something you don't wish to do. Now imagine a stranger or a person whom you do not know properly, pressurising you to something you do not like, can't get worse than that. Closing is also the logical end to a well planned and well executed presentation / call.

How do you close then, what's the right way to close? The answer is that there is no sure shot way or no one way of closing, in fact there are a million ways of closing and only the most 'street smart' will have the skill and ability to make that small adjustment just at the right time, or even convert that big objection into a turning point to close successfully.

The biggest trait

Yes you definitely need to have the basic traits for a successful sales career like communication skills, self confidence, mental ability, analytical skills, aggression, hard worker, ambition, patience, self belief etc in any permutation or combination but the biggest of them all in my thinking is being 'Street smart', that's the one you got to be. That is what will give you the cutting edge and separate yourself from the crowd.

All successful sales people have been street smart and excellent at closing. They have mastered the art of prospecting, identifying needs, handling objections, build trust and find million different ways to close. Their fun lies in making the killing, getting what they want. They operate like skilled hunters and whatever comes their way they go for it and hunt it down. The beauty of successful sales people is that they enjoy closing the most. In fact it gives them a great high and the difficult the close is the more enjoyment they get out of it.

The biggest question

Who should close the call? This is a question which i have asked in each and every sales training session and it is amazing to see that only ten to fifteen percent get that right. So who should close the call is a million dollar question and the one and only answer is:

Always you, always the sales guy

Yes, only the sales person making the call is the one who has to close the call. Never be mistaken, confused or forget that you are the one who has to be in charge. Passengers never drive, drivers drive. You are the driver and command control over the whole machine. You need to know exactly what to push, press or move when.

In fact the bigger, honest fact is the retailer himself looks up to you to close or help close. He looks forward to your confidence to take the right decision. It is your aggression, knowledge, confidence, assurance that makes him take decision. However big & powerful the retailer might be, he definitely needs your confidence to take a call. Try it whenever you want, even if he is absolutely clear about the product & quantity that he wishes to buy but if you tell him that you are not so sure, in most of the cases he will abandon his choice and decision and immediately ask you for a suggestion.

Some in fact consider it to be the most painful part of the whole call, in fact i have seen sales people avoiding to get to the close after the whole call, some even start getting nervous reaching the end of the call. What's the point even making the call then.

When should you close?

The answer is 'Immediately, As soon as you get the buying signal'

So, what is a buying signal?

By definition *'A buying signal is an indication of intention to indulge'*. This means as soon as he starts thinking of making a buying decision he will start indulging in discussions or mannerisms which will indicate his intentions to take a decision. That is the moment you need to immediately capitalize upon.

Some buying signals are

He will pick up the product and start fiddling with it.

He asks about prices or compares it with what he sells

He will ask probing questions (Delivery time, discounts, margins etc.)

Start to bargain or negotiate

Start being friendly with you (Offer tea, a seat to sit, let you in the shop etc.)

Ask for a demo, sample

Ask after sales support or replacement policy

Ask payment terms, credit policy

Asking about satisfied customers or others who have brought

Some buying signals lead you directly to closing point you just need to pick them

1. Let me think about it - He is interested, go for it suggest the quantity.

2. I have already brought for today and can't buy more - He is maybe looking for credit, go for it.

3. I never purchase on impulse or first visit - He is looking for re-assurance, show testimonials or referrals.

4. Business is slow right now - He does not want a big quantity, suggest him smaller quantity.

5. It is expensive - You have not explained the features vs benefits properly, go back to the presentation.

6. Have to speak to father / partner - Cant decide on his own, offer presenting to his father partner (Decision maker).

7. I may not be available when you deliver - He is worried about the delivery, go for it.

You just have to analyze and understand what he actually means and this will come out of experience only.

How do you close

As mentioned earlier there are a million ways to close but it has to be done skilfully so that it seems natural. All successful sales people have their own ways to go about it. But there are some proven techniques that can be applied, which most of the successful sales people do. All you have to do is skilfully analyze as to what the retailer is saying and which technique is applicable there. Any technique applied by you should be made a part of the call and it should seem a natural process.

Let's me share some of the closing techniques with you.

Direct closure technique

This technique is a natural one and should be applied first up. You are in command of the call, the presentation went well, there are no major objections and the atmosphere is positive, go ahead & apply. Do not waste even a second, just go ahead and close.

'So i am giving you 36 pcs. which will be easily sold till i am here next'. As always i assure you of the best of my services. Now having said that you have to quickly move on to the next product or action. If there is no objection your job is done.

Direct close has to come out of your command & confidence about your company, product or services and even the market & the retailer. Most successful sales people use this technique to close as they are absolutely sure of what they are doing.

Alternative closure technique

This technique is applied if you are sure that the retailer will buy but not sure that how much he will buy. Remember that you have to keep in mind that he looks forward to you for suggestions. The product is yours and you are the expert. He never wants to get into a situation where he makes a choice and later it comes back to him. So he definitely wants your involvement in the decision.

So what do you do, give him a alternative without giving him an alternative. How do you do that, now you have decided that you want to sell him 24 pcs, looking at his past purchases and payment capacity. You also know that 36 pcs might be high for him so the suggestion will be 'Do i give you 24pcs or 36pcs'. Now you have given him an alternative clearly knowing that he will not go for the higher one. He will immediately say that 'No, no 36 pcs is high', you have to immediately agree and say, OK' i will go as you say as i always respect your decision, i am giving you 24 pcs then. You have sold your quantity making him feel that he has made the decision. You have sold what you wanted and he has played in your hands.

Physical action technique

This technique is applied when even after a good call and presentation you are not able to judge his intentions to buy. There are also no big objections that you face and you do not know what to do next. He has neither shown any interest or resistance and you immediately need to move on to close.

Take out the order book, tab or whatever you use to take down the order and start putting down his establishment name. Ask for his shop address or phone number or any other minor detail, the chances are that he will immediately react with either a 'Hold on' or start giving you the asked details. Now if he gives you the details as asked consider the call closed as he has brought into your presentation. If he asks you to hold he will immediately reveal his major objection and you can immediately put everything aside and move to the call. Go back to the sales folder and you may have to start again, you might have missed something which now you know and need to explain.

The Sandwich close

This technique is applied when you realize that the retailer is not convinced with the price or value for money of the product. This technique requires you to go back to the call as the price has not been presented at the right moment.

I have realize through my experience of 20 years that in 98 percent of the cases the retailer does not want a low price, all he wants is a fair price, or a value for money price and at the best a competitive price but certainly not the lowest. I have hardly sold anything making it low priced or cheaper than the competition. The moment you lower the price too much he goes into a quality comparison or suspicion mode and you may lose after that. He is concerned if his consumer will find value for money in the product and not give it back to him for being expensive.

Go back to the sales presenter and first share the benefits, sandwich the price between features and benefits and make it look a value for money or bargain preposition. All you have to say is that look such features for just this price and amazing benefits out of which two benefits even competitors also do not have.

The trail order technique

So you have tried everything and nothing seems to work, you still have one last thing left. Fine sir i understand your hesitation to buy my product, so why don't you buy a very small quantity to try it out in your outlet. Please consider it as a trial order and only when it starts moving order more. I am sure if you take a small quantity of 6 pcs and display it somewhere at eye level near you, it will definitely sell. Tell him that this is a request as you really want him to experience the product quality or how easily it will sell. You can also share with him if you have an advertisement support and any other activity that the retailer may not want to miss out on (sampling, visibility etc.) the one consumer that might turn up after seeing the advertisement.

As an alternative do not push a quantity, a scheme or anything, let him only decide the quantity also if need be. The objective is to make the call productive and give him something. This technique is applied when everything has failed and he is not buying into anything. You now have to try one last time to make sure that the call does not go unproductive.

Instant reverse close

This technique is applied when the retailer share's his inability to afford a particular item or states a reason which involves a high cost of the product or service. If he states that, it clearly means that he wants to purchase the product and now looks towards you for solutions to make it affordable to him or put it within his reach.

You have a solution but you first need to take a commitment, then reveal your offer. Inexperienced sales people often make the mistake of revealing their plan or solution first to come to know that now the retailer has another issue and the solution didn't help his problem. Take your time to confirm if this is the exact problem and he will buy if you solve it. Don't jump to provide him a solution or show eagerness to solve his problem, it should in-fact come as a favour to him which will also create respect for you for all future meetings.

'Too expensive' he says and your answer needs to be 'that precisely why you need to buy it'. Suppose i solve your problem, will you buy it? pat will come the reply 'Yes'. Ok then we have a deal, this is the time when you present your solution. 'You want the lowest price' he says yes and the same quality he says 'yes'. Then i offer you the product at this price, the same quality, with another offer of returning it if it is not sold as a bonus. I also offer you a small gift if you display the product in your window as another addition just for you. Now this should be the best time for you to buy this product because you will buy it anyway sooner or later.

For this technique you have to hold on to some additional benefits which you can reveal to him later in the form of a bonus or a favour.

Affordability or counter offer technique

This technique is used if the retailer says that he is not able to shell out the money right now. Look into his past records, probe his payment methods, ask the distributor for suggestions before presenting him a solution.

He says 'I cannot pay now', Ok sir let me see what i can do. Maybe i am able to solve your problem, what i can do is make a provision deferred payment. How about paying half now and the rest in two weeks. If the retailer has a genuine problem you can offer him paying in four equal instalments spread over a certain time period. Make sure that you take your local distributor into consideration before lending a helping hand because if this retailer is a bad paymaster and the distributor later on refuses, you might lose your reputation in the market.

Make promises which stand and you are absolutely sure that you can handle the commitment made.

The testimonial technique

You have noticed & experienced that the retailer needs reassurance to buy, you can share the details of product brought by his fellow retailers by showing your order book, 'See the best shop in your area has brought it too'. Remember what you see you believe the most. You can also share with him if his rivals / competitors have brought. Always keep testimonials & records ready to show to some, they are very helpful in making some tough customers take a decision.

The break / revisit technique

I used it quite often when all was seem to be lost and believe me most of the times i got the sales. So the call is over but you still feel that this guy can buy but there was something wrong in my presenting or closing that killed the call. I want to start the call again but how do i do that. So i ask for a glass of water or buy something from him. This buys me some time and i look for the right opportunity to get back into the call. I have concluded that once the call is over (as per the retailer) he will mostly come out with the right reason for not buying (On a personal note), that is the time when you strike again and start all over. It's a brand new call don't forget and u have all the chances of closing it.

Never answer any question with a small answer i.e. 'Yes' or 'No'. This is your opportunity to re impress upon the presentation. Every single opportunity to go to your presentation should not be missed, do it at every single opportunity available. In fact go one or two steps ahead and address what you may have missed in the initial pitch.

Some examples are below:

Do you deliver on Sunday - Yes

What you should say

Do you deliver on Sunday - Oh you want it on Sunday, Ok, i will get it delivered specially for you.

What is your delivery time - 2 days

What you should say

What is your delivery time - When do you want it, i will make a special delivery do not worry

Do you offer any discounts - Yes

What you should say

Do you offer discounts - Oh Yes, we definitely do in fact today we have a special discount for you. Last time you were looking for something like this. I have given you the same (Cut the bill)

Do you have more variants - Yes

What you should say

Do you have more variants - Yes, In fact i have bigger packs with great discounts which are faster selling and that i offer only to selected counters.

For trainers

Practice some techniques with the participants. do role plays, form pairs, ask some to be retailers and some to be salespersons. Give them situations and questions for different techniques.

Leaving after the call

Another extremely important thing for all sales people to realize. Leave as early as possible once the call is finished. But never leave without a proper thanking note, ever. Leaving after the call has to be re assuring and thankful. It does not matter if you have been able to sell to him or not, if you do not leave properly, consider sales to him in your next visit a question mark.

Always thank him for the time given to you, never leave without a thanks note. If he has shared some feedback or something which was important, make sure to thank him for that too. Tell him anyways that you enjoyed the conversation and his inputs were helpful. No harm in praising him for the knowledge he has shared.

If he has not brought anything from you make sure you still thank him for sparing time to hear you out and tell him that you will return again with better offers and things that may interest him. Make notes of what he desired and you were not able to provide him. Tell him that he is important for you and the visit was insightful to you.

If he has brought from you, reassure him that he has made a good decision. Tell him that you will return next time with more offers from him. You also need to make sure that you tell him that any replacement or after sales service will be efficient. Share company details or your personal number for any clarifications / issues that he may have, this will give him immense confidence.

Records & returns

Never leave without filling your records and returns. Documenting your actions and outcome of the call there itself is extremely crucial. There are many things which happen during the course of the call which need to be recorded immediately as nobody remembers everything after the day is over. Things like special requests (display, hoarding, QPS scheme etc.), reminders of products, payment date, payment mode, supply time and most importantly the stocks ordered make sure you record it immediately there itself on the shop. I am mentioning 2 extremely important documents that you need to fill, update or record after you have closed the call.

The Daliy sales report

This is the most scarce document of the sales representative / executive and is the go to document for every sales person. This humble document is the most important tool for any organization to record its own market intelligence. One can make important note in this, mention important things like replacements, distribution etc. This document if filled religiously by the field force can be the true picture of the market situation and can help the organization take big decisions. This is used to record the day's visit record, sales orders, distribution, productive calls, total calls and special requests. In today's times the hand held or the mobile has taken it's place but the document & it's importance remains the same. It is an immensely powerful tool for every serious ales person and can generate unbelievable analytics.

Daily route call plan (DRCP)

Another extremely important tool and i have seen the benefits of this myself. All good companies have this implemented and there are standing instructions to their field force to work with this. This document is also used a direction to plan your day from the first call to last one. By this document you clearly know the history of the retailer and the pattern of his purchase. In many a cases this also becomes the DSR and the go to document. This document goes one step further to the

DSR and gives you a detailed description of the activity of the shop / outlet over the past many months to enable you to make a effective call. This is a document which records all previous purchases, displays given, special schemes availed, payment pattern etc. If you have filled this one religiously every time you have the *'Brahmastra'* against the retailer to make the call.

Miscellaneous small tips

Your should always complete your decided no of calls for the day, all calls not attempted is business lost for sure.

Make a proper presentation every time you visit, every call to the same person / retailer is an opportunity to re-register you & your product in his mind.

Never assume that he knows about the product & features, maybe he had some perceptions or may have forgot, all that will be cleared or reinforced today if not previously.

Business lost today cannot be recovered ever, it is lost forever, so get it today. Your effort should be to close the business planned for the day, come what may. Go that extra mile, make that extra call, find a new outlet, go back to the call you could not make/Complete.

Remember every day is a fresh new day with new opportunities and possibilities, you can start all over again with the same enthusiasm and energy as today can be one of the best one's so far.

Never perceive or assume anything, whenever in doubt just 'ASK'.

For Trainers

Do a simple exercises with the group as below for showing him the power of missed calls

Example:

Total calls to be made daily - 35

Total calls to be made in a month - 840 (In 24 days of market working)

Made total calls - 720

Missed calls - 120

Average business per call - R. 250

Average productivity - 45 percent

Productivity lost on missed calls - 48

Business lost - 12000

So they can see the business they have lost just by not making those calls. This is keeping everything else constant. This business lost cannot be recovered also.

Chapter 7

The Eighth Unofficial Step, Merchandising

'Whatever is visible to the customer, has the best chance to sell off first'

In my opinion the importance of merchandising in retail businesses is immense and as per my twenty five plus years of experience the most important reason for the need to merchandise is to engage, inspire & to encourage possible customers to buy more of the products you want them to, increasing your sales, margin and return on space.

Merchandising is an amazing tool and powerful beyond your thoughts. It has to be treated & performed like a religious ritual. Any sales guy who leaves without performing this ritual is doing injustice not only to his employer but to himself too. A well merchandised product increases many fold the chances of it being sold. There are organizations who pay heavily for making sure that the product is well in front of the customer. It can truly set you apart from your competitor. Go to any retailer and see the power of merchandising. The best established brands are the most likely ones that you will see once you enter any retail outlet. In spite of them being the best they make sure they still are visible first, that's why they are the best.

A nice, bright, colourful & innovative display acts like a silent salesman in your absence in the retail outlet. It not only pulls the attention of the customer but also reminds him / her of the product. It also acts as that reminder of the TV commercial that you may be running or that newspaper advertisement that you have given. It creates a brand recall and pushes the customer to pick it up.

A sizeable amount of money of any established organization goes in developing the unique and innovative merchandising material, printing it and transporting it to the point of sales (POS) for merchandising. Companies which realize the importance not only keep a track of the same but also assure that there is a separate team to do this professionally.

Some extremely popular means of display material are posters, banners, danglers, stickers, shelf strips, display stands, counter top dispensers etc.

All successful sales people always carry some handy merchandising tools with them. They realize the importance of merchandising and make sure that they do it before leaving the outlet. Maybe you don't have much merchandising material today but you can always correct, repair or restore that valuable stand, dispensing unit that you gave him last visit.

Some innovative merchandising material that you can develop yourself always

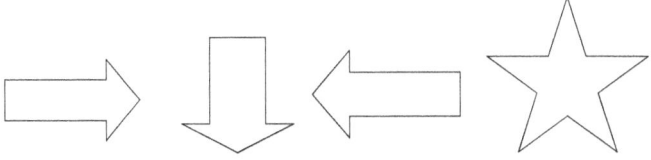

Arrows & Stars can be found at all stationers or can be cut out also. Just keep a permanent highlighter with you always and write anything on them and just stick them. They can also be used to point out at the product location and come in very handy.

Any sales person who values the importance of company merchandising material will always be held in high esteem by the company and even the retailer.

Never use the merchandising material as rough paper, the retailer will do the same.

Never use the merchandising material for wiping hands etc. It is degrading the organization & your own worth (He who does not respect company assets cannot respect anything).

Don't underestimate the retailer, whatever he says he always respects you for the professionalism that you show and respecting your company merchandising material is definitely one of them. He watches you constantly and evaluates you by your actions. If you misuse your own company merchandising material, don't expect him to keep that valuable poster / Dangler / Sticker after you leave.

Where & how to merchandise

I will now share some basics of merchandising with you

- Never start merchandising without the permission of the retailer - Do not forget that it is his establishment and he is the boss. You have to make him a partner in maintaining the display otherwise it will be gone as soon as you are.

- Always make sure that he buys the need to merchandise - If he doesn't buy the need he will pull it down once you leave or not maintain it for you. He needs to understand that you are doing this to increase 'His' sales. If you are able to sell him that it's a favour you are doing for him he will respect you for that and even make sure that the display stays

– You have to make sure that you decide in advance where to merchandise - Do it during your observation step as having pre-decided helps you position it and sell accordingly. Or during a stock check by the retailer during the call.

– Merchandise always at eye level -That's the natural angle for all to see, anything above or below might be a tricky one. Anything done below the waist or above your head is a waste. Out of sight out of mind.

– The closer to the retailer the easier to dispense - Have you ever noticed that whatever is the fastest selling or he wants to sell (for whatever reason) is at an arm's length to him. The closer to him the easier it is for him to dispense or recommend.

– Never clutter your merchandising, keep it simple and clean - If there is too much at display at the same place the consumer ignores it or is confused. You have to be clear what message the display gives to the consumer. The clear

& clutter free the display is the easy it is for the consumer to take a decision. You need to separate a stocking from a display.

—   Make sure that you have clarity with the product or service to be merchandised - Ideally it is the range (to show the variety) or it is a single product (To bring focus) or it is a single product (as it is newly launched), your message and focus has to be absolutely clear. All your merchandising material has to convey the same message. All good companies have a plan-o-gram for merchandising. It is based on the need of the hour or as per focus products.

—   Never merchandise at an unstable place - If you have not merchandised your goods or services at a stable place in the outlet consider it a waste of merchandising material and your effort. Chances are that will not be there for long. Merchandising on mobile assets in the outlet (Door, shutter, window panes, refrigerator door, Elmira etc. should be avoided). I have seen extremely expensive merchandising material lying in the ground or garbage bins minutes after the hard work done, only because it was put at a place which was not stable, what a waste of a great effort and beautiful merchandising.

- Always keep tools handy to make sure that the merchandising is stable and looks good. You have to use certain tools for merchandising (Cello Tape, double side tape, stapler, glue, hammer, scissor, duster, drawing pins, permanent markers, highlighter's, tacker gun). Many companies which know the importance of merchandising tools make sure that they provide the same to their frontline sales team. If not provided by the company make sure that you carry some on your own. These are your ammunition for the war, keep them sharp & handy.

- Merchandise only after you finish the call - Never discuss or attempt merchandising between the call. Do not start to merchandise during the call as it is a big driver of attention. This will take away the build up of your call to closing and kill the call. Only once you finish your call and have closed, go for merchandising.

- Never forget to thank him once you are done - Being thankful is extremely important and more important than that is making him feel important. Even if he has not ordered anything you need to thank him for letting you merchandise. Do not leave any opportunity to thank him or be grateful that he gave you his precious time to present and also let you merchandise.

— Keep displays fresh & be innovative - You should be constantly researching new ways to display differently, you will not only be appreciated but benefit for being different. Whenever you travel to a new town, check in the local shops to pick up new ideas. You can't let your displays become stagnant. You must be constantly updating and changing them to keep customers interested. The retailer wants this too and will be pleased if there is someone who does not come to 'only sell'. While arranging other products in the category, go the extra mile and arrange the other products too (So that someone does not disturb your arrangement when he does the same), he will be grateful and pleased.

— Match product categories & displays - Avoid displaying food items with non foods and vice versa. You can also share your views with the retailer and inform him of such matters. It is extremely important to match the displays with the category. For example if your products belong to the impulse purchase category, it is best that you place them at the checkout counters or behind or near the retailer.

Types of Displays

Window displays - Window displays are an very important part of merchandising. In-fact it is so important that not only there is a separate budget allocated annually by most of the top FMCG companies but also they have specialist agencies doing it for them on a regular basis. A huge and attractive window display is the biggest tool for garment retailers to draw customers into the shop. You have to make them interesting enough to encourage people to go for the products or at least enquire about them. Window displays should pique customers' interest and make them want to explore a little further by asking about the products as mentioned.

One expensive mistake you can avoid is putting something in your window that is susceptible to fading or sun damage, if your store frontage is exposed to direct sunlight. You have to make sure that you or the retailer keeps rotating these products otherwise you are in for some damages coming your way. You need to have proper backing sheets and other matching POS material to make it thematic and well directed to the target customer.

Check-out counters displays - These are extremely important for companies who sell products which fall in the impulse purchase category. The world over the checkout counters are the most coveted ones and you will find the best companies worldwide acquiring them (Gillette®, Duracell®, P&G, Cadbury's, Wrigley's etc.).

Category displays - These displays are basically done in the category itself. Each company is assigned some space to display their range, in fact the premium companies have negotiated to acquire a certain percentage of the category share as per market share or the kind of dominance they wish to have. The top companies make sure that they have definite 'plan-o-gram' for their range in line with their sales & marketing strategy. Having a plan-o-gram and displaying the products accordingly is the best way to ensure off takes in a certain direction.

Created opportunity displays - These are displays created out of unused space i.e. shelf edges, shelf headers, hanging dispensers, special dispensing units etc. Many companies spend a lot of money to develop such display units so that they don't have to pay for space to display their products. Again Gillette® is the best example and one of the pioneers in this field and has created many cutting edge & winning display installations for extremely diversified formats of outlets.

Floor Sales Unit

This is an independent sales unit stationed specially for the intended company with special promotions or a new product launch. Standing apart from the category in a place where it attracts maximum attention is the purpose. Usually they are a part of the special promotions by the store or specially paid for display units by any organization. They are installed with a proper plan-o-gram and at times are also specially manned by promoters to bring the extra focus required or sample the promotion.

Contrary to what many brand owners believe, consumer behaviour research continually demonstrates the most effective way to generate brand visibility, introduce a new product and encourage sales is by focusing on the tried-and-true method of in-store merchandising. It is a fact that almost 76% of purchasing decisions are made directly in the store and this is true even for non impulse purchase items. Moreover, the importance of point-of-sale appears to be rising always, whatever many may think about the changed scenario with internet & e commerce the percentage of decisions made in the store always remain high. Organizations are spending millions to develop new creative ways to display their products in the store. A Nielson study found 72% of the individuals surveyed discovered new products while they were in the store.

Merchandising is still one of the most powerful tool to ensure steady off take and will remain till the retail stores exist.

For Trainers

Trainers can go to the market and click some pictures of each type of display and show them. Also click pictures of where not to merchandise and show to the group. Click pictures of different types of display units too and show to the group. I have avoided pictures as i did not wish to show any brands.

The Two mantras / chants of an F.M.C.G. salesman

Distribution. Display

Distribution.Display, Distribution.Display,
Distribution.Display, Distribution.Display,

Keep chanting these and it will make you successful. Any corporate or individual if diverts himself from this *mantra* may find it hard to succeed. Whatever is distributed well and displayed well is what has the best chance to sell out and succeed.

Memorable - Some important awards

Best Regional Performer Award from **Sanjeev
Khanna**, Executive VP Sales (India), Glaxo
Smithkline (Ex Head Spl. channel, Kellogg's UK

Receiving Top Performer (North) Award from **Manoj Kumar**,
MD India, Glaxo Smithkline (Ex.MD P &G, Australia & NZ)

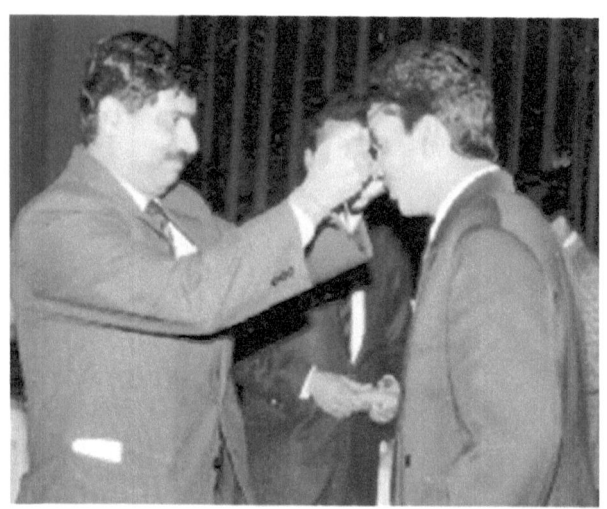

Receiving Best Sales representative award (1992)
from **Rajeev Tandon**, Director CIS Countries,
SC Johnson (Ex VP sales, Gillette® India)

Receiving the Best Sales representative award (1991)
Ranu Kawatra, Ex President & CEO, Pearson
India, Ex Sales director Duracell® (P&G India)

Receiving the Outstanding ASM award (1999) from **Vivek K. Sehgal**, Sales Director, India Sub continent (Henkel, India)

Receiving the Top Performer award (1993) from **Ian M. Kirk**, MD Gillette® India

Meeting the worldwide CEO's

Welcome & interaction with then Duracell® worldwide CEO &
President **Charles R. Perrin** during his visit to India Nov, 1994

With **Jeff Van-der-Eems**, Worldwide CEO of United
Biscuits HQ in Hays, London, July, 2014

My living room many a times served as
a training & meeting room too

High personal involvement of the then MD & VP at micro
levels - The frontline & the frontline sales team was so very
important for them, Sitting on my right is **Pradeep Pant**,
President Asia Pacific & EEMEA, Mondelez International
(The then MD Gillete India) & sitting on my left is **Rajeev
Tandon**, Director CIS Countries, SC Johnson, Ex Director
India & SW Asia, Gillette® (The then VP Sales, Gillette® India)

With my Sales team, Gillette® India launch - 1993
Check the innovative unit (supply
vehicle) mounted razor dummy

Merchandising Kit

Marker Drawing Pins Double Sided Tape Cello Tape

Tacker Gun Stapler Screw Driver Scissor Plaas Hammer

Sales Merchandising Kit. A good salesperson is
always ready and has all required tools at hand

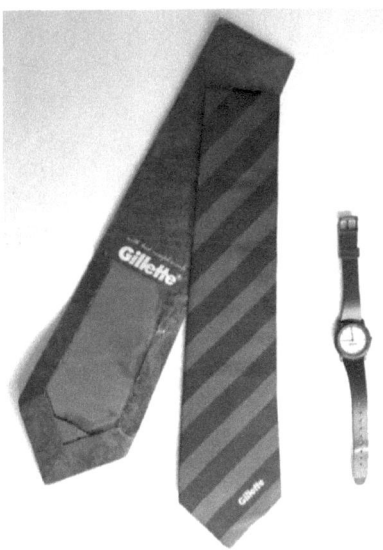

The first look, first impression is crucial - **Gillette's**®
Tie & wrist watch... *The best a man can get*

Launching a premium tea brand as **Head of Sales & Marketing**, along with **Pankaj Kapoor**, MD Harrisons Malayalam Ltd (RPG Group).

Options Infinite (OISPL):
Adding Value to Retail Business

The traditional Indian Retail industry is an extremely dynamic market place where products, customers and markets are continuously evolving. As a result of this evolution there is prevalent change in the brand marketing, approach to services and above all consumer approach. Amidst such a revolution taking place in the Indian retail industry, targeted distribution and pin pointed coverage are the key words to avoid the clutter and reach the right customers. While a good product is an essential to start with, it's even more critical to place the product in the right outlets. Irrelevant direct distribution not only requires huge investment but also is a sheer waste of energy, effort & resources if not controlled.

Innovating, Evaluating, Implementing

Based in Delhi, Options Infinite Services Pvt Ltd (OISPL) has emerged as a pioneer in retail data & consulting domain. "In a country with over eight million outlets, how to start and where to start from was our biggest question. We started with

the FMCG vertical, biggest and the most challenging one. We developed a unique model to connect with ex-FMCG personnel all over the country which worked wonders for us. Today OISPL maintains a robust database of over 1 lac FMCG outlets spread across 22 towns in India, along with 10,000 outlets of kids, salons & garments" speaks Rajul Chaturvedi, Principal Founder Promoter and Chief Creative Officer, Options Infinite Services Pvt Ltd.

Options Infinite offers "Real time" market information which enables organizations track key distribution, find gaps, achieve distribution, plan launches, plan manpower, coverage and much more. Since the information offered is not extrapolated from small samples as in the case of the traditional research firms, one can be very precise, targeted & highly effective in execution. "At Options Infinite, we offer a single platform of data, consulting and servicing which no one else has. Data, Intelligence, solutions all in one place, is what differentiates us from our competitors", articulates Rajul.

Robust real time data also had a solid foundation for a 360 degree consulting platform. From launching new products, devising marketing strategy, creating market infrastructure, handling day to day sales operations, training, audits, market research, OISPL does it all. "We are now proud to be India partners for some top companies from UK, Swiss & South Africa for their India operations", he adds.

The Big E commerce Bite

OISPL is the 'only' company in

● Rajul Chaturvedi
Principal Founder, Promoter & COO

India providing exclusive content to e-commerce players in the grocery space. OISPL carries a huge database of 40,000 FMCG sku's with elaborate details. Some of the leading e-commerce players are its clients. OISPL not only provides content but also helps in acquiring the retailers for few e commerce players which is a unique proposition.

Infinite is Where you Can Go

OISPL has been around for some years but recorded impressive growth since its new avatar in 2014 & now boasts of some very prominent Indian and MNC clients. Enlightening on the future road map of the company Rajul concludes, "We maintain a database for over 1 lac FMCG outlets which we plan to take up to 1.5 lacs & 50 towns by end 2016. The bigger plan however is to expand our unique data model to new verticals i.e. Paints & hardware, Pharma, Footwear, Stationery, White goods and garner a bigger chunk of retail data. We want OISPL to be the one-stop-shop for real time data & consulting services in the traditional trade space." ∎

> OISPL maintains a robust database of over 1 lac FMCG outlets spread across 22 towns in India

Featuring in Retail Consultants Magazine, Aug 2016 - Rated one of the top 25 fastest growing consulting companies in India

All Pictures courtesy Rajul Chaturvedi's private album

Chapter 8

The Training Perspective

You have a training department or not i am sure that after reading this book and comparing your situation you will surely feel the need to debate for one. What is the role of sales training in an organization? Is it just "good-to-have" or a "must have" for an organization? Is it an indulgence of the management whenever the budget permits or it is a part of its conscious strategy to achieve organizational goals? How sales training is perceived really depends on the organization. There are organizations that think it is really a waste of time and that sales team learn best while doing their job. Then there are other organizations that invest a lot of time and money to train their sales team. Let's examine how important it is for organizations to impart training to their sales force.

Sales training can help aspiring salespeople develop and practice the skills they need to succeed and increase their confidence level. Some salespeople have a tendency to focus solely on the "people" aspects of the position, such as prospecting and making sales calls, while overlooking the administrative tasks. Effective sales training points out the importance of functions such as tracking daily activities, keeping accurate records and analyzing reports. This information can help the salesperson better manage their time, increase organization and determine areas that need improving. Hence the sales team needs to be trained on various aspects of business i.e. product knowledge, administrative aspects, procedural compliances, soft skills & business ethics.

There are a lot of extremely talented sales people available who would love this role. But you need to select people who do it with passion and not as a function in which they have been moved or for the time being. You need people with a teaching mentality and who love to work on this and keep it updated with fresh examples and ways to share this with the different people that they train.

Motivation

The ability to do work and to do it willingly with a desire to excel are two different aspects of a sales job. The ability to do work is obtained with the help of good education and skill training and willingness to do work with a desire to excel and improve constantly, is only obtained with the help some kind of motivation. Willingness is more important in comparison to ability as that infuses the extra energy to be ahead of the rest.

A sales training department is also extremely helpful in motivating the team to raise their standards of performance or at least maintain it. Motivation improves efficiency & the efficiency of a person is reflected through increase in productivity and decrease in costs. Motivation is one of the most important aspect of the whole exercise. If you do not ensure a motivation plan in place, employing educated and qualified people may also not give results.

Some organizations and entrepreneurs do not think that motivation of a sales employee is 'that' important or important at all. If they do not make sure about this aspect, they are bound to lose some good employees. Good performers need motivation and average performers can be transformed into good performers by the right kind of motivation. Be reminded that there will be many sales people who do not get motivated by money only, they need other forms of appreciations or motivation to keep them going.

Motivation can come in many forms i.e. Money is one of the best, so make sure that there are enough incentives but money only may not suffice as there will be people who look for other things. So the other forms of motivation may be as below:

1. Written appreciations / Certificates etc.

2. Prizes / Gifts

3. Additional responsibilities

4. Involvement in strategy making and other important things.

5) Constant / Regular interactions or communications.

6. Direct access to anyone for any issues / problems.

7. Being realistic to issues and situations.

So train, motivate, review, train again, motivate

So there are two approaches to training employees

1. The Classroom approach

2. The Market approach

The Classroom approach

Ask the group to do a simple exercise and list the issues that they face. Ask them to list themselves the points they need to improve upon

Discuss and diagnose the issues that you need to work upon. Select 3 most crucial one's to start with as you cannot concentrate on more than that, the rest can be take care of the next time.

Share with him / her the same and prepare a plan of action. Share tips on how he should approach and put a recording process in place. Monitor the progress by constantly reviewing the progress.

Next time when you meet, discuss the 3 aspects which needed improvement, share the progress and if all is well, give him / Her the next set of points of improvement to work upon.

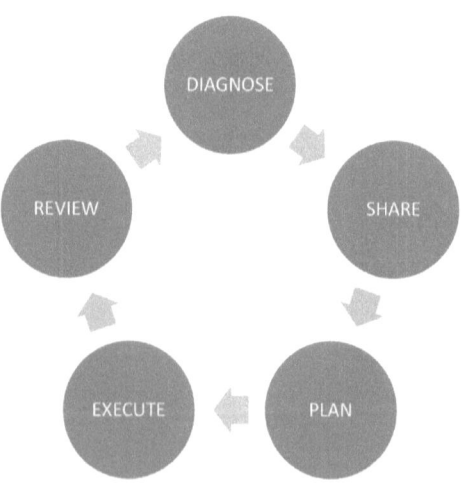

Classroom sessions are boring for sales people who have an habit to move around and meet different people day in day out. Make the sessions interesting, make animated slides, introduce some humour, ask them to repeat what you said. Make sure that the sessions are interactive, hence the suggested role play will make it interesting and also break the monotony of a classroom session. In organizations where they do not have a full fledged training department this can be done jointly by the HR department & the concerned manager / supervisor.

The Market approach

So the theory will not work if it is not executed verbatim practically & the market is the best place to do it. So market working with him / her is the best way to demonstrate the theory.

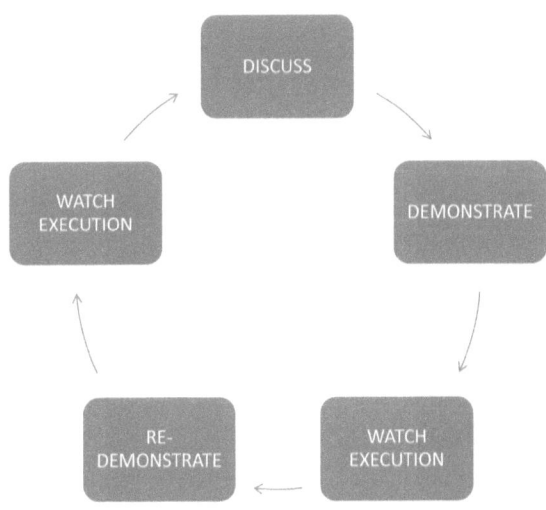

So now it's time for the real action, the market execution. You now need to remind him / her of the points to be taken care of or work on. Make 1-2 demonstrations of a call you wish him to make. You can also pick on specific calls where you can demonstrate the execution of issues that he is facing.

Now ask him to make a few calls, don't interrupt (In fact never interrupt between the call), let him make mistakes, don't worry about the call being unproductive just let him carry on and you make the notes. Once he finishes and you are out, share the things that he did right & share the things he needs to work on or improve.

If you feel that he is still not confident make another couple of calls and demonstrate what you were impressing upon. Let him make the mistakes again and keep making notes. At the end of the day share a summary for the day with him.

You need to give him one contact each month for the next 3 months and then at the end of it evaluate him on the three points you decided to work upon.

The approach of a trainer is suggested as below:

1. Review the call

2. Review the result achieved

3. Share what he executed with finesse

4. Discuss what could have been done better

5. Set small goals

6. Share possible solutions (If he can't think of any)

7. Let him choose the one's he thinks he can easily execute

8. Create an action plan with him

9. Share monitoring mechanism

10. Decide review dates

In organizations where they do not have a full fledged training department this can be done concerned manager / supervisor during his market contacts.

Trainers need to develop specific material of themselves to show during theory sessions. That not also makes it interesting but also helps make the session more interactive. Remember you have to make it a involved and interactive session and the group should enjoy every bit of it.

Chapter 9

Knowing your Channel & Partners

So how does a product reach it's end consumer.

It's important for every sales person to know some basics as that is so very important for him. He must know the basic and broad process as to how the supply chain works. I am mentioning below a simple chart for all to have a look and understand the process of a product reaching the end consumer.

A TYPICAL SUPPLY CHAIN CHART
OF ANY F.M.C.G. COMPANY

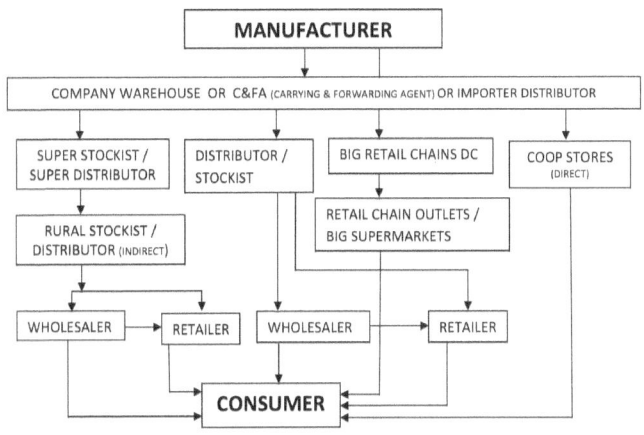

STOCKIST vs DISTRIBUTORS

They are typically the same thing in India depending upon the terminology used by the organization. In India any well established company would have a 1000 to 5000 or maybe more stockist depending upon the product & category it is in or the amount of direct distribution it wishes to indulge in. Each town / city may have one and the larger one's would have more than one. In India there are more than 10 million outlets and servicing them is a huge challenge, hence there are various modes and many intermediaries for any product to reach a consumer.

In India the unorganised or the traditional trade outlets form a larger chunk of the entire retail paraphernalia. A distributor / stockist in India caters to smaller retail universe in a small geography (Within 5-10 Km max or 400 to 1200 retailers), that is called direct distribution. He may not service the larger chain formats called Morden trade (i.e. organized retail) or cooperative stores. He does not have a large sales force of his own and relay's on the company manpower to push sales and cover his area. Indirect distribution (Whole sellers selling to very small and petty retailers or consumers) is also large and one cannot do without it. So in the smaller universe that he covers and services directly he may be servicing three times more retailers than perceived due to indirect distribution.

In other places outside India a distributor typically is appointed for the whole country and caters to the entire country retail universe and all formats available in the country. The multinational giants know that on their own, they cannot master local business practices, meet regulatory requirements, hire and manage local personnel, gain intelligence & introductions to potential customer hence a local distribution. Having a local distributor channel breaks the whole buying and selling process and all its related negotiations into manageable tasks, each performed by entities that specialize in certain skills. So a distributor of any company in most of the countries would receive goods directly from the company manufacturing the products and distribute all across the country either directly or thru smaller entities in his country depending upon the market scenario of the country. It is simpler than India as the retail trade is mostly organized and they have to deal with fewer entities. They have their own sales force which sells for them multiple brands and multiple companies. They also have their own marketing team to make sure that they keep up with market promotions and expectations of the companies they distribute for.

Why is a distributor essential- what is he for?

A distributor's primary job is to service the market well & efficiently!

Why are all these layers needed in distribution? Why can't a manufacturer directly sell to a retailer, who can sell to a consumer? It's a fair question, and in some cases, that may also happen. But the fact is that many producers are either too small or too large to handle all the necessary functions themselves to get their products to market.

To put it in another way this is a win win situation for both the players (company and the distributor). A distributor cannot create a brand which has a consumer pull and can sell on it's own. On the other hand the company cannot open its own warehouses in the smallest of towns to sell to consumers directly, hence a distribution module.

Can you imagine the manufacturer collecting money from 4-5 million retailers, not possible. Similarly using an importer distributor for any country, for example, can be handy because they know the laws and customs of the suppliers' nations; and they generally offer their own lines of credit so the retailer won't have to deal with currency exchange or negotiate payment terms with a bank in another country. Finally and extremely crucial it is easy to pull out of the market with the least liabilities.

Can you ever imagine a consumer buying its monthly grocery needs directly from the manufacturer, not possible, hence the layered system.

A good distributor is like a solid backbone of the business in that area / country. If you get a stable and solid distributor half of your job is already done as you can be rest assured that your goods will reach in time to the retailer.

The three primary essentials to appoint a distributor

So what do you look for when you are appointing a distributor for your company? There will be many factors and it can be a topic of debate but in my opinion we need to look into & evaluate three primary factors before deciding for anyone. The distributor needs to have three basic things for being eligible to be appointed as a distributor;

Manpower

He needs to have adequate manpower to service his area. When i say that i mean manpower to supply goods, sales team to take refill orders, managers to look after the warehouse, logistics & manpower to maintain accounts, records & returns. You don't want a single man army there as there are too many functions to do at a distributor side. You don't want one man loading, dispatching, counting, billing and also selling. You need a proper team to take care of various functions so that everything runs smoothly.

Infrastructure

He needs to have the requisite infrastructure in place, i.e. a proper office to operate, warehouse to store goods properly, cold storage (as per products needs). I Ie also needs to have his own vehicles to supply goods to the retailers and the market.

Finance

Finally any distributor who does not have enough finances to invest in the business will not last long. He has to be financially stable and be having at least 2-3 stable distribution businesses already. If he operates on too many loans, he may collapse any day leaving you stranded with debits to be realized. A thumb rule 'new business, fresh investment'. His ability to invest fresh capital in a new business is also indicative of his aggression and risk taking capability, after all there is no safe playing in this business.

All the other things are additional and can be looked as mentioned below

1. Market reputation - Is he regarded well in the market.

2. Trade relations - Does he know his retailers, specially the big ones.

3. Brands / companies handled - Does he have some reputed top brands with him.

4. Credit in the market - Does he allow adequate credit terms in the market.

5. Personal attributes - Is he a supportive person and has progressive attributes.

6. Other factors - Does he have additional businesses is his family also involved in the business (Father, son or other family members etc)

7) Personal involvement / commitment - Is he devoted to the distribution business or is this

his 'other side business'. Does he give enough or equal time & attention to all other business.

8. Company / Firm constitution - What kind of a firm he has (Proprietor firm, Partnership, Pvt Ltd., LLP Etc.) which gives you a further idea of his stableness & longivity.

But if he is missing any of the three primary essentials, he should be avoided as he may not be the best bet for your business. Don't be in any illusion or be confused, just rate any of the distributor on these three parameters first and then look into the other sub factors mentioned above (1-8) before taking a call as appointing 'Anyone' will not last long mark my words.

Finally don't let him choose you, you need to choose him as you want the best.

Chapter 10

Way Up the Ladder

Invest in yourself

Investing in oneself in any way is giving yourself more chances to grow and stay ahead of others in today's extremely competitive atmosphere. Nurturing, caring and investing in both your mind and body allows you to have more to give now and in the future, more energy, more knowledge, more compassion, more ideas, greater strength, physical and mental endurance. Investing in yourself truly makes a difference in your life, your well-being, and your ability to thrive and perform to the best of your ability. The extent to which you invest in yourself, mind and body, not only shapes the way you interact with the outside world, it often reflects the opinion you have of yourself. Your future is in large part determined by your willingness and ability to invest in yourself now.

Make a list of personal goals and the means to achieve them, follow that. Set up immediate, short term, future and life goals and constantly review them. Work on creating resources to achieve them, do not lose sight of them. Never forget that you have to invest in yourself to get them. Investing in yourself emotionally, physically, spiritually and financially, will allow you to become the best version of yourself. When you are the best version of yourself, you will be an attraction to many.

Advance your education -

A formal education (Graduation in any stream) is extremely essential in today's times, if you are without one you are most probably missing that one big chance which you might get someday. Go for that additional degree which gives you specialization in a certain field / subject. Go for that specialization, this is the time of specialization and it will almost certainly give you the edge if there is a chance in the current organization or elsewhere. Indulge in short courses from time to time. Times are changing fast and technology is increasingly making fast inroads, you do not wish to be left out. Keep learning and updating yourself whenever you get the opportunity or sense that it is required now. There are many part time classes available or you can also enrol thru online learning mediums today and study online, give exams online.

Train yourself (Use available resources or find one) -

There will definitely be training programs conducted by your organization, don't miss them. Keep the presentations go thru them and practice in details. Go for training programs / workshops conducted by other experts, whenever you can. This will also give you the opportunity to meet and interact with individuals who are like-minded. Be in touch with the trainers, ask them for updated information or anything new that they develop. Show eagerness to learn and everyone will be more than happy to have an eager student. Constantly discuss new avenues to learn from your seniors or who your admire in your organization.

Expand your knowledge base

Today's world is a constantly changing world, if you are not updated with the latest changes, you might be missing out on a career chance. There is so much to learn around in today's world and so much of information available with so many mediums. There are books, newspaper, journals and the mother of all the internet. The most simple and effective source for knowledge is your daily news paper, read as much as you can. Pick up subjects which interest you, find the literature, go to the net, organize a debate. Get to the base of your products, ingredients, origin of them, find their history and you would be better off than most of your colleagues. Sharing knowledge makes you loved and respected amongst not only by colleagues & peer's but also amongst the trade fraternity. I have personally experienced it and found it so exciting. I had customers / retailers who used to wait for me to know more or discuss certain topics or even take advice, sales followed automatically.

Explore your creative side-

Please discover yourself, there is a creative side to all of us but most of us do not make any effort to explore it. Either we are too lazy or just plain ignorant about it. Creativity is that pass to unearth the millions of possibilities which you cannot know otherwise. It opens so many doors in personal and professional life and helps you to view your problems and available solutions with a totally different angle. I feel that whatever i have achieved today is also because i was able to think different and many a times come up with solutions that were out of the box and always gave a new dimension to the situation in hand. I was appreciated and stood out as everyone looked forward to me for something different and innovative each time we had a situation. Note it down, creativity can be the catalyst in the manifestation of continual learning and lifelong activity. It allows us to be inspired, have fun and appreciate the beauty in the world.

Learn a new language

The world is shrinking and boundaries are being broken. Go to any developed country or see all around you, you will find mixed cultures, races, nationalities and a new world which is much more progressive and growing much faster than you realize. Look within your own country there are so many languages, dialects and ascents to learn. Languages brings you close to people faster than anything else. The moment you start speaking in the native language of an individual the whole perception changes and a certain comfort level comes in.

Go travel

So don't be a frog of the well, go around and see the world, there are so many things to be learnt which you can never ever get to know if you stay in the same place. I have travelled all over the world and believe that it has really widened my perspective to another level. Travel really opens you up to people, cultures, languages, nature and many more things. I was able to think & act differently and my creativity has an edge as i have seen something work somewhere and when implementation here, it worked wonders, which i would never would have thought off had i not travelled out and seen it myself. Venturing into the unknown gives you courage, power to explore and also to test the real you.

Indulge in any sport or hobby

Get back the soccer / cricket sessions, that badminton or table tennis game that you enjoyed playing. Pick up that brush that you abandoned and indulge in the painting that you once were good at. Plan for the trekking, running or swimming indulgence that was such an important part of your growing up. Get up, be physically active and sweat it out it will give you immense satisfaction. It removes the fatigue, the frustration, the dullness, the monotony that work schedules get you to. No doctor can heal you better, go indulge, don't miss them.

Adopt to change - This is a whole vast subject in itself and has many books, articles, debates, speeches available all over. In fact there are many motivational speakers who make sure that they dedicate an entire session to this topic. Change is basically having the ability to be able to move from one situation to another (mostly a situation of comfort). For some people change is usually brought about by a desire to want to change or do something different, but it's something that we all need to recognise if it is to happen. Without change we are less likely to have a go at new things or do things differently. We will more than likely shop at the same grocery store; eat the same foods; and paint our houses the same colour. We will also stop ourselves from learning and experiencing new things and changing so that we may become better people. Change helps us grow in a progressive manner.

*'The simple fact of the matter
is that the only constant in our
lives is change, only change is
permanent. it is bound to happen'*

I remember seeing a laptop for the first time in 1993 and realizing 'man that's really going to change things and if i don't get to learn using this machine i am going to be outdated soon' i thank my stars for that. I made sure that i spend 1 hour every day or alternate day (whenever possible) to learn it from the boss's secretary and it paid me dividends. After some years I had a particular boss who didn't like me for my aggression and creative approach (As my suggestions and achievements were applauded many a times) but fortunately did not know how to use computers & had to rely on me for reports and other analysis as computers had become important and a must. Once i started making his reports and helping him out with his analysis, not only did i learn how things work as a manager but i also became one of his most trusted aides.

Today changes are happening much faster than you can even imagine and come to know about. Resisting to change or ignoring change brings in lot of insecurities. You start to suffer from lack of information, depending upon opinion of others, less confidence in your opinion and ultimately taking wrong or even detrimental decisions. Your decisions become adulterated and you may most probable take a wrong one.

Gone are the days of people working in the same organization for more than 15-20 years or an organization making one big change every 36 months. People are making aggressive decisions & organizations are facing faster, more complex, more interdependent people and making cross-functional changes faster than ever before. Being able to deliver results on multiple changes allows an organization to achieve their strategic vision and thrive in today's changing landscape. Similarly people changing from a engineering back ground to hospitality or from an FMCG career to a telecom company are quite common.

Chapter 11

The Conclusion

Your attitude is the single biggest factor in making you a successful person and taking you where you want to go in life.

The mindset by which you approach will determine its outcome than any other element in a sales call or life. That frame of mind makes you energetic, gives you courage, makes you smile, makes you positive, makes you confident and all that shows during the call converting it into a powerful and effective presentation.

Your own belief system alone can determine your fate. You have to believe in the organization, your team, your superior, your products and above all yourself. Believe in it or don't be a part of it. Even small successes help and every success strengthens your belief system. Finally the broader your success history, the deeper your self-belief system becomes.

So the conclusion is

'A born salesman' is a myth, selling is a science which is an acquired skill and need to be developed by hard work & application'

The fundamentals need to be in place, firmly.

Your attitude is the difference between success and failure, get a positive attitude.

Establish long term relationships, they will take you far.

Be honest and speak the truth always

Be fully prepared for any situation.

Go for it rather than wait for it to come to you

Always look professional, that's where you earn from

Finally, be helpful.............don't try to sell and disconnect.

Remember only hard work succeeds, there are no shortcuts in life.

Whatever you do, do it with passion.

Acquire knowledge, it always helps

As mentioned already if you are not able to sell yourself, it's quite likely that you may not be able to sell the product / services as well.

How can you fail

- If you don't have the right (positive) attitude

- If you don't believe in strong basics of the business

- If you don't embrace failure

- If you don't believe in yourself

- If you don't believe in the organization you work

- If you can't get along with your team, every time

- If you don't stand by your word's / promises made

- If you don't believe in a disciplined life

- If you are lazy and don't believe in sweating it out

- If you don't stand up for something or are known for something.

To sum it up, 'You are the reason yourself'

&

Your goal is simple - To be the best sales guy, rest will follow

I am sure that this book and the contents can help any type of sales person by way of valuable insights to create his own modified sales call according to his field and the type of call. Today is the age of internet & Google, presentations are moving to tablets and hand held devices. Reporting is also moving to handheld devices connected to the trade partners and the organization. But what remains unchanged is the human interface and i am sure that this book will give its readers enough insight to manage that.

I wish all my readers & sales trainers a successful sales career, i will be the happiest person if i have been able to make even a tiny difference to even 'one' sales person to be a successful sales person or sales trainer.

Thanks to all my readers for buying this book or even reading it till the last.